The Story of Glen Eden Lutheran Memorial Parks

David P. Stechholz

Copyright: Text @ 2023 by David P. Stechholz

Major editing, ISBN number, and page layout by the Rev. Joel Baseley

Major editing by Mr. Thomas Habitz, Sr., General Manager Emeritus, and Mr. Ernie C. Fackler III

Additional editing and considerable assistance from Mr. Craig Zitterman, Glen Eden Memorial Parks General Manager

FIRST EDITION

Glen Eden Memorial Parks, Livonia, Michigan

Printed by Sheridan Books, Chelsea, Michigan

Unless otherwise indicated, Scriptural quotations are from the ESV Bible (The Holy Bible, English Standard Version), copyright @ 2001 by Crossway Bibles, a publishing ministry of Good News Publishers. All rights reserved.

Cover design and layout: Curtis Jackson, Digitalliance (Glen Eden West panoramic scene). Title page - Spring, 2022, Garden of Victory, Glen Eden Lutheran Memorial Park, Livonia, Michigan). Non-copyrighted pictures, unlicensed, have been used.

Stechholz, David P., 1948 --
    God's Acre: The Story of Glen Eden
    Lutheran Memorial Parks
    (An Abbreviated Version)
    154 pages

ISBN – 979-8-9902894-1-3

Printed in the United States of America

Contents

i	Title Page
ii	Copyright Page
iii	Contents
v	Dedication
vi	Preface
viii	Glen Eden Staff
x	Timeline
xvi	Prayer
Page 2	Chapter 1 - The Beginnings of Glen Eden During the Great Depression and World War II
Page 16	Excursus – A "Glen Eden Story"
Page 22	Excursus – The Fackler Family's Dedication to Glen Eden
Page 28	Chapter 2 – Financial Security and New Development
Page 30	Excursus – Glen Eden's Neighbors (Other Cemeteries)
Page 39	Excursus – Glen Eden Lutheran Church
Page 42	Chapter 3 - Glen Eden during nationally tumultuous Years – The 1960's-Mid-1970's
Page 52	Chapter 4 – The Years Following the Detroit Riots
Page 57	Chapter 5 – The Late 1970's & 1980's: Moving in a Different Direction

Page 58	Excursus - The Backbone of Glen Eden – The Faithful Maintenance Crew
Page 65	Excursus – Pastor's Point and the Garden of the Reformation
Page 67	Chapter 6 – Farmington Hills Property Sold – Glen Eden Starts a New Era with an Enhanced Image
Page 69	Excursus – Wildlife at Glen Eden
Page 79	Chapter 7 – A New Millennium and a Leap of Faith – Beginning of Glen Eden East
Page 86	Excursus – Involvement in the Community
Page 89	Chapter 8 - The Changing Nature of the Cemetery Business: Glen Eden Makes Improvements, Reaching Out By God's Grace
Page 98	Excursus – The Halboth Family – Another Family's Legacy of Dedication
Page 108	Excursus – The Habitz Family – And Still Another Family's Dedication to Glen Eden Lutheran Memorial Parks
Page 111	Chapter 9 – A Near Century of Service
Page 119	Bibliography
Page 122	Glen Eden Lutheran Memorial Parks - Glen Eden General Managers, Board Chairmen, Current Board Members
Page 130	Committals at Glen Eden
Page 133	Maps
Page 135	Scriptural Passages

Dedication

To Janet,

my beloved wife, whose future grave and present grave marker we share in Pastor's Point at Glen Eden Lutheran Memorial Park West, Livonia, Michigan, and with the marker's Scriptural words:

"Glad songs of salvation are in the tents of the righteous."

Psalm 118:15 (ESV)

**The Monument of Victory (I Corinthians 15)
Glen Eden West at Christmastime, 2023**

"May God be gracious to us and bless us and make His face to shine upon us, that Your way may be known on earth, Your saving power among all nations. Let the peoples praise You, O God; let all the peoples praise You."
– Psalm 67:1-3

Preface

This is an abridged version of the larger, detailed book, **God's Acre: The History of Glen Eden Lutheran Memorial Parks.** It is meant as a popular read. It contains no footnotes, deferring for detailed information to the larger work cited. Quotation marks are occasionally used, but without reference (see the larger volume for citations). The unabridged version was written from the perspective of the Minutes of Glen Eden Board of Directors, Annual Delegate Meeting' Minutes, and interviews. This shorter volume has condensed that material while retaining most of the pictures. The detailed listing of names and events is found in the former book, but not this shorter version. Yet the flavor of Glen Eden's vast history and an abbreviated timeline are retained.

Glen Eden Memorial Parks will soon be celebrating 100 years of service to our area of greater Detroit, Michigan. Centennials and even near-centennials are powerful times of remembrance for a church, any godly organization, and for a cemetery. Glen Eden is commemorating nearly a century of service as a niche in God's Kingdom of Grace, His Church, especially in the Evangelical Lutheran Church in North America. In particular, the founding congregations and pastors of the church bodies of these humble portions of "God's acre" could not have envisioned the depth of God's continued blessings to Glen Eden.

Glen Eden is how members of Evangelical Lutheran congregations and the greater Detroit area know these memorial parks (cemeteries), which are now three memorial parks and a columbarium. **First and foremost, we give all honor and praise to the Lord, our God.** It is He who has blessed and guided the memorial parks, the association of Lutheran churches, and the faithful men and women with ability, leadership, and vision over the century. These faithful include General Managers, Staff, and Board of Directors. **Secondly, we are grateful to the founding fathers**, the boards of directors, and the general managers, as well as sales personnel, office and maintenance staff who, over the years, have ably overseen God's resources to grow and expand this hallowed ministry. **Thirdly, we are grateful to the families** of various Christian faiths, especially Evangelical Lutheran families, who have entrusted to us the care of the mortal remains of their beloved who have fallen asleep in Jesus and await the great Day of Resurrection.

And finally, we of Glen Eden value life, a gift of God. We uphold the sanctity of human life from conception to grave. To that end, we have memorial markers in our cemeteries that honor the lives of the unborn and of children who died in the womb or in infancy. It is a humble honor for us to have written this "history" of the Glen Eden story.

In the Name of Christ Jesus, the Resurrection and the Life,
The Rev. Dr. David P. Stechholz
December 6th, anno Domini 2023 †

The Board of Directors and General Manager Craig Zitterman of Glen Eden at the Annual Board Christmas Dinner, December, 2022. Our wives join us for this annual dinner.
See pg. 119 for the most current picture of the Board.

Glen Eden Staff

Left - Glen Eden General Manager, Mr. Craig Zitterman, in front of Administrative Office Building

Right – Glen Eden West Grounds Superintendent, Mr. Greg West, from Service Bldg. toward cemetery

It is nearly impossible to get all of the Office and Grounds Maintenance Staff together for a picture. They are all over the grounds and/or taking turns working on a Saturday. Over the years they have exhibited true dedication to Glen Eden!

Previous page (below) – Glen Eden West Office Staff: left to right – Kathy Mueller, Chris Kitzman, Janette Walters, General Manager Craig Zitterman, and Eric Moore Missing, but pictured separately, and working on a Saturday: Lee A. Wilson.

Pictured above – Glen Eden West Grounds crew: left to right – Chris Fulkerson (uncle of Matt), Terry Cupp, Gerald Fontaine, and Matt Fulkerson. Pictured separately – Matt Fulkerson.

Pictured by green maintenance vehicle – Matt Fulkerson, and Terry& Maurice Cupp (brothers). Missing from these pictures, Greg West, Grounds Superintendent (see previous page).

Timeline

1929 (Jan. 16th)	**Glen Eden Development Company**, as a private stock company, **organizes** for the purpose of selling shares for a cemetery
1929 (Oct. 29th)	Stock Market crashes, start of **the Great Depression**, lasting till World War II
1930 (Feb. 7th)	Glen Eden **Lutheran Cemetery Association (LCA) organizes** as the Lutheran Division of Glen Eden Memorial Park; incorporated for the purpose of purchasing cemetery sections
1930 (Oct. 26th)	First burial – Rev. John M. Gugel
1931 (Sept. 27th)	Glen Eden dedicated as a cemetery at the site on Baseline Road in Wayne County
1932 (Aug. 21st)	Name changed to "**Glen Eden Lutheran Memorial Park**"
1933 (July 20th)	LCA Board of Directors sign an agreement with the Glen Eden Development Co. to acquire the Glen Eden Memorial Park
1933 (Oct. 29th)	First annual Memorial Service at Glen Eden
1934 (May 15th)	24 Lutheran pastors representing 23 congregations met on cemetery grounds
1937 (Aug. 12th)	No funerals allowed on Sundays, Memorial Day, Christmas, or New Year's
1938	Construction of Glen Eden Carillon Tower (later taken down years for the construction of the Mausoleum and Chapel
1940 (Dec. 6th)	498 total burials at Glen Eden to date

1941 (Dec. 7th)	Japanese attack on Pearl Harbor; the U.S.A. enters World War II
1945 (June 3rd)	Memorial Service with Lutheran Hour Speaker, Rev. Dr. Walter A. Maier (I), as homilist. 1,000 cars, 5,000 in attendance
1945 (Sept. 2nd)	World War II officially ends in Tokyo Harbor. The war ended in Europe in May, 1945
1946	Toilets and wash bowl facilities added
1948	Christmastime grave blankets popular during preceding, and following decades
1950-1952	Glen Eden's "turn-around," as sale of graves greatly increases
1951	Survey of Cemetery boundaries completed
1955	Beginning of efforts to dissolve the Lutheran Cemetery Association and get new charter
1956 (Feb. 10th)	Announcement made at Annual Meeting **that complete ownership achieved of Glen Eden Lutheran Memorial Park** (title secured, January 17th, 1956) – 174 acres
1956 (May 25th)	Fire destroys the Service (Maintenance) building; new building completed, 1957
1957 (Jan. 2nd-3rd)	Glen Eden Memorial Association dissolved (different than LCA). A milestone year: final liquidation of old indebtedness

1959 (Mar. 26th)	State of Michigan approves dissolution of the Lutheran Cemetery Association and grants a **Charter (Articles of Association) to Glen Eden Lutheran Church** (as an ecclesiastical corp.), owning & operating Glen Eden Lutheran Memorial Park).
1960	Purchase of 79-acre Evert Farm on north side of Eight Mile Road, Farmington Twp., Oakland County. Approval of the purchase date back to 1957.
1961 (Jan. 14th)	Dedication of the "new" Office Building, by the lake, and an "open house" to community
1964	Purchase of 140-acre Franjac parcel, adjacent to cemetery
1965 (May 14th)	Adoption of new Constitution and Bylaws for Glen Eden Lutheran Church
1974 (June 2nd)	Dedication of first part (center section, with Chapel of Memories) of the Glen Eden's Mausoleum-Chapel (additions came later)
1981	A very young Craig Zitterman begins working in maintenance at Glen Eden; becomes Grounds Superintendent (1993-2019) and later General Manager (2019-present)
1985 (Nov. 10th)	Dedication of second part (1st addition) of Glen Eden Mausoleum
1986	Beginning of efforts to sell Glen Eden's Farmington Hills property
1986	Glen Eden Enhancement Project begins

1990-1991	Construction of the entryway Arch into Glen Eden Memorial Park
1990-1991	Construction of new Glen Eden Administrative Office building (Dedicated on June 2nd, 1991, along with the Arch & Entranceway as part of Dedication and Patriotic Memorial observance)
1992	Sale of Glen Eden Farmington Hills property to City of Farmington Hills for a sports park
1995 (Oct. 22nd)	Dedication of the Luther Statue in the Garden of the Reformation
1997	Glen Eden Grounds crew unionized
1999 (Oct. 3rd)	Dedication of third part (2nd addition) of Glen Eden Mausoleum and the Fountain Plaza (directly behind the Mausoleum)
2001	Board approves start Glen Eden Lutheran Memorial Park East in Macomb County
2001 (Sept. 11th)	Terrorist Attack on the United States (commonly known as 9/11)
2003	Glen Eden honored, recipient of the 8 Mile Road Boulevard Association Beautification Award (awarded again in years following)
2004 (June 13th)	Dedication of Glen Eden Lutheran Memorial Park East in Macomb
2004 (Sept. 10th)	47 acres sold of Glen Eden West property to Golf Ridge Properties, LLC for 118 detached condominiums for $4,080,000

2005 (May 29th)	Dedication of Glen Eden West's second mausoleum, the St. Gabriel Mausoleum, after construction began in June, 2004
2005 (Nov. 6th)	Dedication of Glen Eden Columbarium at Lutheran Church of the Redeemer, Birmingham, Oakland County
2013	Dedication of the Garden of Grace (cremation garden) at Glen Eden West cemetery
2019	Dr. Calvin Kaiser (deceased) wills property and assets to Glen Eden for starting a new cemetery in St. Clair County on his land
2020	COVID-19 Pandemic
2021 (Jan 6th)	Assault on the Capitol in Washington, D.C. over the results of the 2020 Presidential Election
2022 (June 3rd)	Dedication of the Crucifix statuary, Pastor's Point, Glen Eden West
2023 (June 10th)	Dedication of Glen Eden Lutheran Memorial Park St. Clair

Picture of the Plaza waterfalls and columbaria, looking toward the back of the Mausoleum-Chapel.

"O Lord, our Lord, how majestic is Your name in all the earth!"
–Psalm 8:1

Prayer

✠ In the Name of the Father and of the Son and of the Holy Spirit. Amen. ✠

Almighty God, Lord of the living and the dead, by the death of Your Son, Jesus Christ, You destroyed death, by Your rest in the tomb You sanctified the graves of Your saints, and by Your Resurrection You brought life and immortality to light so that all who die in Him abide in peace and hope. Bless, we humbly pray, Glen Eden Lutheran Memorial Parks that these hallowed grounds – "God's acre" – may be resting places for all who have fallen asleep in Jesus until the Day when You waken and clothe them with incorruption and immortality. Be with those who lay their loved ones to rest in these memorial parks and columbaria, and comfort them in the hope of the resurrection of the body and life everlasting. Strengthen our faith that at the appointed time we may peacefully fall asleep in You and be gathered with all Your saints in light; through Jesus Christ, our Lord, who lives and reigns with You and the Holy Spirit, one God, now and forever. Amen.

"So teach us to number our days that we may get a heart of wisdom." - Psalm 90:12

✠   ✠   ✠

"For the wages of sin is death, but the free gift of God is eternal life in Christ Jesus our Lord." - Romans 6:23

St. Gabriel Mausoleum and First Responders Memorial at Glen Eden Lutheran Memorial Park West

To the
Glory of
God

Chapter 1
The Beginnings of Glen Eden During the Great Depression and World War II

Reflect for a few moments on a few of America's famous cemeteries. They have important names: Arlington National Cemetery in Arlington, Virginia; the National Cemetery in the Presidio overlooking the Gold Gate Bridge (San Francisco Bay); the notorious Boothill Graveyard in Tombstone, Arizona; Oak Ridge Cemetery and the tomb of President Abraham Lincoln, Springfield, Illinois; the Pilgrims' Burial Hill, Plymouth, Massachusetts, dating to 1622; Trinity Churchyard in Manhattan (New York City); St. Louis Cemetery, New Orleans, Louisiana; and, Gettysburg National Cemetery, Gettysburg, Pennsylvania.

A book worth glancing at is *Over My Dead Body: Unearthing the Hidden History of America's Cemeteries*, by Greg Melville, published in 2022. While it does not mention but a few church-related cemeteries, it provides a significant overview of cemeteries and memorial parks in the United States. It adds a perspective, albeit mostly secular, that cannot be overlooked, including segregated African-American cemeteries in America.

In short, take time when traveling about the United States and elsewhere in the world to walk through cemeteries, memorial parks, and burial grounds. Children and youth should also be taken to these hallowed grounds to learn respect and reverence for life and for the dead, while gaining a wealth of historical knowledge and appreciation for the lives of people who have gone on before us, the current living.

What's in a Name?

Names are significant. People are remembered by their names, and as Christians, they are known by their faith in Christ Jesus and their righteous deeds. The same is true of cemeteries and memorial parks. There is much importance to Glen Eden's name. There is a matchless name, though, that of the Lord Jesus Christ.

> *"Therefore God has highly exalted Him and bestowed on Him the name that is above every name, so that at the name of Jesus every knee shall bow, in heaven and on earth and under the earth, and every tongue confess that Jesus Christ is Lord, to the glory of God the Father."*
> - Philippians 2:9-11

The Name of Jesus is exalted. Jesus is King of kings and Lord of lords. Salvation is through Him. Jesus is the Lord, the eternal Son of God. By virtue of His name, Christians do not take the names given them at birth for granted. When parents name their posterity, thought and care goes in to the naming of their child.

The name of "Glen Eden" is significant. How it was chosen for the small, original memorial park on Baseline (Eight Mile) Road in Livonia Twp., Michigan, in 1929, is not known. Clearly, it was chosen from the Garden of Eden, the earthly paradise found in the first book of the Holy Bible, Genesis.

The Lord God planted our first parents – Adam and Eve – in the Garden of Eden. It was Paradise on earth. There was no sickness, sorrow, pain, or fear, except of course the fear (holy awe) of God. They lived in a perfect relationship with their Creator. Their fear of God was a holy reverence of their Creator, who provided them with everything.

We know the all-too-tragic story of the fall of man (humankind) into sin in the "saddest chapter" of the Holy Bible, Genesis 3. Adam and Eve fell into sin, having been tempted by Satan, the old Evil Foe, who took on the form of a snake. We know the rest of the story from Genesis Chapter 3. Adam and Eve were expelled from the earthly paradise – the Garden of Eden – by God. Yet in His infinite love, He would send His beloved Son, our Savior and Lord, Jesus Christ, to redeem lost and condemned souls.

Why would this biblical account belong in a book about a beloved memorial park? First the biblical Jewish conception of a "garden" was that of an abode of the blessed. Even with death, the result of Adam's sin (original or inherited sin), comes the necessity to honor life, the life of our friend or loved one of the family with a proper committal. Hence the need for memorial parks and cemeteries (also called graveyards or burial grounds).

Who actually came up with the name *"Glen Eden"* prior to 1930 remains a mystery, lacking any documentation. An earthly "glen" is often used as a place of tranquility, a valley often with gently sloping sides, derived from the Scottish usage of valleys or glens in the Highlands of Scotland. Melding the word "glen" and "Eden" into Glen Eden as a "name" directs us both back to the original Garden of Eden and our first parents. It also points ahead to the heavenly Eden, the Paradise of the elect, the home of believers in Christ, our Savior. Simply put, the name Glen Eden carries biblical weight and the certain hope of that eternal Eden through Christ Jesus.

The entrance into Glen Eden Lutheran Memorial Park East – 26 Mile Road, Macomb, Michigan

The Founding of Glen Eden

From time immemorial, believers in the Lord God and His holy Word have honored their dead, whom they esteemed in life. They gave them a resting place of honor and marked that place accordingly. Throughout North America, there are hundreds of thousands of cemeteries and memorial parks of different types and sizes, some still in densely populated cities, some in remote, rural areas. Many were established by churches of all different faiths, not to mention community, family, and private cemeteries, national military cemeteries, and those of Native American and non-Christian religions. In North America, Evangelical Lutheran Christians would usually plant a cemetery adjacent to or close by the church building. Of course, that made it very easy to have the funeral in the house of worship and then for the pallbearers to carry the casket of the deceased to the nearby cemetery, "God's acre," as it used to be called in many of the old Lutheran rites of burial.

Throughout North America there are hundreds of Lutheran "church cemeteries," usually in rural or formerly rural areas. In short, one could find a wealth of knowledge and Lutheran history in North America in visiting Lutheran cemeteries, whether the larger ones that became renowned in larger metropolitan areas or the small, sacred "God's acres" nearby large or small rural Lutheran churches. If you are in the Midwest, consider visiting St. Lorenz Evangelical Lutheran Cemetery in Frankenmuth, MI; Concordia Cemeteries in Fort Wayne, IN, and St. Louis, MO, Bethania in Chicago; and especially Glen Eden Lutheran Memorial Parks in greater Detroit (Livonia, Macomb, and St. Clair), which is the subject of this book.

An earlier picture of the entry into Glen Eden West (Livonia) from the 1960's

Glen Eden – Begun in 1929

Glen Eden's beginnings as a Lutheran cemetery may have had some roots prior to 1929. Until recently in 2023, the masthead of Glen Eden Memorial Parks' website read: "Founded in 1929 by a small group of Lutherans, Glen Eden Memorial has served the needs of Christian families with the highest standards of individual care and understanding." Naturally, though, there is more to the story, or should we say "history." Today Glen Eden consists of three memorial parks and a columbarium:

- Glen Eden West in Livonia, MI
- Glen Eden East in Macomb, MI
- Glen Eden St, Clair in St. Clair County, MI, and
- Glen Eden Columbarium, Lutheran Church of the Redeemer, Birmingham, MI

The beginning of Glen Eden Memorial Parks dates back to January 16th, A.D.1929. At that time, a group of dedicated men organized the **Glen Eden Development Company**. The early Minutes of what became Glen Eden Lutheran Memorial Parks are sketchy. This may well be true of many cemeteries. Some individuals may have had in mind the creation of a Lutheran cemetery association prior to January 16th, 1929. Both the Development Company's Board and the later Lutheran Cemetery Association's "founding fathers" in 1929 and 1930 respectively had numerous meetings to acquire property at a rural area on Baseline Road (later known as Eight Mile Road) in what became Livonia, Michigan. The Incorporation Articles were filed on January 17th, 1929. On February 27th, the stock issue of 44,990 shares was validated by the Michigan Securities Commission for the purpose of giving one share of stock with each section sold. A section was four grave plots. The original stockholders purchased one section of the acquired property, paid in cash to the Glen Eden Development Co.

140 Purchase Agreements were dated prior to the **Stock Market crash of October 29th, 1929**, often for several sections. Interestingly, on March 16th, 1930, Gethsemane Evangelical Lutheran Church of Detroit purchased ten sections (40 burial plots) for $1,450, to be paid in 24 payments monthly. Another interest item was the purchase of 11 burial plots by the Bethlehem Evangelical Lutheran Church Ladies Aid Society of Detroit on July 14th, 1930. Many of the Purchase Agreements in 1930 were by women. Also, several purchases of sections were made by syndicates in 1930 and 1931, the word "syndicate" having a different, legal meaning back then than it does in the 21st century.

Start of the "Lutheran Era" and the Lutheran Cemetery Association

On February 7th, 1930, the **Glen Eden Lutheran Memorial Association** was incorporated as a stock company for the purpose of purchasing sections for use as a cemetery for Lutheran people of the synods and their congregations that were a part of t**he Evangelical Lutheran Synodical Conference of North America**. At that time and in the greater Detroit area these would have been congregations, primary of the Evangelical Lutheran Synod of Missouri, Ohio, and Other States (Missouri Synod, later LCMS) and the Wisconsin Evangelical Lutheran Synod (WELS). The Evangelical Lutheran Synodical Conference of North America was a federation of six confessional Evangelical Lutheran synods, established in 1872. By 1930, the Missouri and Wisconsin synods were the two largest of the four remaining synods still in the "Synodical Conference."

From its inception, the Association only wanted to develop a part of the land owned by the Glen Eden Development Co. as a Lutheran cemetery, but that would later change. The names of the first officers of the Glen Eden Development Co. should not be forgotten as the wonderful "pioneers": **Frederick R. Robinson**, President; **Arthur Dove**, Vice-President; and **Ernest C. Stieler**, Secretary and Treasurer. The "Lutheran" identity did not exist at the cemetery's beginnings in 1929, but it would become so in the next few years.

In tracing the roots of Glen Eden Lutheran Memorial Parks, it is important to recognize the year of 1930. First, both the Missouri Synod (1847) and Wisconsin Synod (1850) were originally German speaking. The names of both synods (in English) were "The German Evangelical-Lutheran Synod of Missouri, Ohio, and Other States" and "The First German Evangelical Lutheran Synod of Wisconsin." Geographically, they were not limited to Missouri and Wisconsin, though eventually their headquarters or "centers" became St. Louis and Milwaukee. Both were confessional, immigrant German Evangelical Lutheran church bodies with challenging, if not difficult beginnings. Detroit area churches of the Synodical Conference were largely Missouri or Wisconsin Synods, though smaller confessionally Lutheran church bodies were also represented, including the National Evangelical

Lutheran Church (Finnish) and the Slovak Evangelical Lutheran Church (SELC).

In the 1930's, the Missouri and Wisconsin Synods had congregations that were still using German for worship, meetings, and their parochial schools, though most had become English-speaking or used both languages. From the outset, the founders of Glen Eden conducted business in the English language, though a stilted English, as the hand-written Minutes reflect a German script. The acculturation process that involved immigrants would often involve second and third generations adopting English as their *lingua franche*, and even more so their children, though pastors would more readily cling to the German mother tongue. The United States entered into World War I in 1917. In that year, the German Missouri Synod changed its name, dropping the word German ("Deutsche") and changing the title to English. Yet in 1919, after World War I ended, almost two-thirds of the German Missouri Synod still used German as the primary language of worship. In the next 20 years (1919-1939), and just prior to the United States' entry into World War II, the Missouri Synod did a language flip-flop. By 1939, two-thirds of the Synod's churches were using English as their primary language of worship.

The Great Depression

Glen Eden's initial roots go back to January, 1929, but it was not till **September 27th, 1931 that the cemetery – Glen Eden Lutheran Memorial Park – was dedicated** in a Service at its Livonia Twp., Michigan location on Baseline (Eight Mile) Road, a few miles west of Clarenceville, one of a few communities within what later became Livonia (1950). In the Service of Dedication of **30 acres of what was known as "The Lutheran Division of Glen Eden Memorial Park,"** 6,000 people were present. One can hardly imagine such a large crowd gathering today for an initial dedication of a cemetery.

This took place in the wake of the Stock Market crash on "Black Tuesday, **October 29th, 1929**. On that single day, Wall Street investors traded some 16,000,000 shares on the New York Stock Exchange. Billions of dollars were lost, wiping out the investments of thousands of stock investors. This plunged the industrial world into what became known as the Great Depression. It would take a decade and another world war before countries and investors started to re-emerge from bankruptcy and economic disaster.

Glen Eden was born in the middle of the worst economic time in United States history. It was solely by the grace of Almighty God that Glen Eden came to exist, no less survive. Many of the early meetings of the Lutheran Cemetery Association were held at the Parish Halls of either Gethsemane, St. Matthew's, or Bethlehem Evangelical Lutheran Church in Detroit. The Minutes were often hand-written, though some where typed (with a manual typewriter, sic!) and often from the office of the Association's Secretary, Funeral Director Henry C. Schatz on Livernois Ave., Detroit.

The **first recorded Minutes** (February 7th, 1930) stated that a meeting at the Hall of Gethsemane Evangelical Lutheran Church was called "for the purpose of organizing a Lutheran Cemetery Association. **The following congregations were represented:**

- Gethsemane Evangelical Lutheran Church, Detroit
- Nazareth Evangelical Lutheran Church, Detroit
- Zion Evangelical Lutheran Church, Detroit
- St. Matthew's Evangelical Lutheran Church, Detroit
- Holy Cross Evangelical Lutheran Church, Detroit
- St. Paul's Evangelical Lutheran Church, Farmington (today, Farmington Hills, and re-named Shadow of the Cross)
- Atonement Evangelical Lutheran Church, (Fordson) Dearborn
- Bethlehem Evangelical Lutheran Church, Detroit
- Mt. Olive Evangelical Lutheran Church, Detroit
- Calvary Evangelical Lutheran Church, Lincoln Park, and
- Christ Evangelical Lutheran Church, Rouge River.

These men, were elected officers by acclamation:
Rev. Herman Metzger, President - Pastor, St. Matthew Evangelical Lutheran Church (Cabot at Michigan Ave., Detroit)
Mr. Fred L. Wulf, Vice President – Layman, Nazareth Evangelical Lutheran Church (Vicksburg at Grand River Ave., Detroit)

Rev. W.O. Kleinhans, Treasurer – Pastor, Calvary Evangelical Lutheran Church (now in Lincoln Park)
Mr. Henry C. Schatz, Secretary – Layman, Zion Evangelical Lutheran Church, Detroit, and
Mr. George F. Otte, Sales Manager.

14 recorded Board of Directors meetings were held in 1930. Also added to the Board of Directors, in addition to the above-named officers were **Mr. Victor Ketterman**, Christ Evangelical Lutheran Church, Rouge River; and **Mr. Harry Meister**, St. Stephanus Evangelical Lutheran Church, Detroit.

The great dedication of the "founding fathers" is so apparent. By 1932, the Lutheran Cemetery Association had an office at 715 Griswold Building, Detroit. The Glen Eden Development Co., represented by **Mr. P.B. Warr**, had its office in Detroit. Warr served as General Manager; he was often invited to attend Association Board meetings. The first meeting of the Association at the Glen Eden Memorial Park grounds on Baseline Road was the regular meeting, held on Sunday, August 21st, 1932, at 2:30, with a "Luncheon" served at 6:00 p.m. **In that same meeting, the name was changed to Glen Eden Lutheran Memorial Park.**

The original company - Glen Eden Development Co. – had no specific Lutheran identity. It was caught up in the woes of the Great Depression and could not meet its financial obligations. One of its officers persuaded the Glen Eden Lutheran Memorial Association to entertain the idea of obtaining the cemetery as a Lutheran burial ground. On July 20th, 1933, a group of individual Lutherans agreed to sign a contract to purchase the park (in its entirety). In paying off the Glen Eden Development Company for $240,000, the Lutheran Cemetery Association would then sell 2,700 sections (a section equally four burial plots) over a period of eight years. At that time the Association further agreed to purchase another block of 26 acres from Mr. George Stuckey for the price of $18,200. If the records are correct, this would then have brought the total acreage to 136 acres. When all of the $240,000 was paid off, the Association would then acquire the deeds to the land, all personal property of the Glen Eden Development Co., and the

Cemetery Permit. But with the Great Depression, it would take two decades for this to become reality.

By October, 1933, there had been over 40 burials and over 300 sections sold. The first annual Memorial Service was held the afternoon of October 29th, 1933. The annual Memorial Services became an important part of Glen Eden's emerging history.

The Tower in Glen Eden, a landmark for many generations of visitors to the cemetery, was erected in the late 1930's during the Great Depression. It was the duty of the Grounds Superintendent to "stand guard" when there was a burial service or a special event.

"The name of the Lord is a strong tower; the righteous man runs into it and is safe." - Proverbs 18:10

The Vision of Glen Eden: *"The Most Beautiful Lutheran Cemetery in America"*

What was the vision, the goal in terms of the founding of the Glen Eden Lutheran Memorial Association? The obvious vision was to develop a beautiful Lutheran memorial park by engaging the congregations. The Lutheran congregations would be engaged, without obligating them financially, as members of the Association to sell burial sites to members of their congregations (of the synods that constituted the Synodical Conference). This helped reduce indebtedness and establish a perpetual care fund. Every burial site that was sold would result in the person's congregation receiving a commission of $25. By November 13th, 1937, there had been 252 burials at Glen Eden Lutheran Memorial Park.

But back to 1933. **These are the 24 Congregations that had become members of the Lutheran Cemetery Association:** (D. = District; * no longer in existence; if LCMS only, then a congregation of the Michigan D.)

- Atonement Evangelical Lutheran Church, Dearborn (LCMS)
- Bethlehem Evangelical Lutheran Church, Detroit (LCMS)*
- Calvary Evangelical Lutheran Church, Lincoln Park (LCMS)
- Christ Evangelical Lutheran Church, Rouge River (LCMS)*
- English Evangelical Lutheran Church of the Covenant, Detroit (LCMS-English D.)*
- Emmanuel Evangelical Lutheran Church, Dearborn (LCMS)
- Epiphany Evangelical Lutheran Church, Detroit (LCMS)*
- First Slovak Evangelical Lutheran Church, Detroit (SELC/(LCMS-SELC D.)*
- Gethsemane Evangelical Lutheran Church, Detroit (LCMS)*
- Holy Cross Evangelical Lutheran Church, Detroit (LCMS)*
- Mt. Hope Evangelical Lutheran Church, Melvindale (today, Allen Park, LCMS)
- Mt. Olive Evangelical Lutheran Church, Detroit (WELS)*
- Nativity Evangelical Lutheran Church, Detroit (LCMS)*
- Nazareth Evangelical Lutheran Church, Detroit (LCMS)
- Pilgrim English Evangelical Lutheran Church, Detroit (LCMS – English D.)*
- Redford Evangelical Lutheran Church, Detroit (LCMS)*

- St. Andrew's Evangelical Lutheran Church, Detroit (LCMS – English D.)*
- St. John's Evangelical Lutheran Church, Detroit (LCMS)
- St. Matthew's Evangelical Lutheran Church, Detroit (LCMS; later, in a micro synod)*
- St. Paul's Evangelical Lutheran Church, Farmington (Farmington Hills, LCMS)
- St. Paul's Evangelical Lutheran Church, Northville (LCMS)
- The Evangelical Lutheran Bethel Congregation of Detroit (LCMS)*
- Unity Evangelical Lutheran Church, Detroit (LCMS)*
- Zion Evangelical Lutheran Church, Detroit (LCMS, later, LCMS– English D.)

It should be acknowledged – however painfully – that 15 of the 24 congregations of the Lutheran Cemetery Association are no longer in existence. Yet their history and contribution live on through Glen Eden Lutheran Memorial Parks. At the February 18th, 1933 Lutheran Cemetery Association (LCA) Annual Meeting, held at Gethsemane Evangelical Lutheran Church's Parish Hall, 23 delegates answered the roll call, with eight proxies being entered. (At the end of this book is an abbreviated listing of various General Managers, Officers, and Board members.) In a February 18th, 1933 letter to the congregations and pastors of the Lutheran Cemetery Association, Board President Meyer wrote:

> We are very much pleased to report very satisfactory progress of our noble project – "Glen Eden Lutheran Memorial Park." The spirit and faith of the Glen Eden Development Company, as evidence by the manner in which they have cooperated with us in the development of our property, is indeed commendable, especially so under present business conditions which have not been very favorable. They have shown their faith in us. By all means we should reciprocate to the best of our ability.
>
> If you are purchasing a Burial Site on our installment terms, it will be very helpful to our cause if you will make it a special point to keep your Contract in good standing through the prompt payment of your monthly installments. It means much

to us and to the success of our project – *your project* (italics added – ed.). We are very determined to make it **THE MOST BEAUTIFUL LUTHERAN CEMETERY IN AMERICA** and we shall succeed in that. (capitalization in the original letter; bold, added – ed.).

The Glen Eden Lutheran Cemetery Association had resorted to deficit financing, but the result was that it succeeded. Congregations and their parishioners came through. Lutheran congregations were not directly solicited for money. However, burial plots (sections) were purchased by their parishioners. Regular and special Board meetings often reported on sales of debenture bonds, balances of capital stock shares, adding a cross and other cemetery decorations, notations of thanks for out-going Board members and other officers, as well as difficulties with certain individuals, and encouragement to pastors to having their congregations send in their applications for membership in the Lutheran Cemetery Association. In addition, in later Board Minutes, it was reported that Pastor Metzger had apparently gone to the Evangelical Lutheran Church of St. Lorenz, Frankenmuth, MI. It was noted by him that a cash collection was received from generous folks there in the amount of $2,150.

Pastor's Point was made ready for use by September, 1933. In a Lutheran Cemetery Association Letter of September 30th, 1933, to the pastors of the congregations of the LCA, President Edward Meyer stated: "Mr. Elmer Garchow, our superintendent, has the plat of Pastors Point ready. First come, first served." (The term, "plat" is no longer used. It simply meant a map or a chart of a subdivision of land.) Added also was encouragement to drive out to Glen Eden and see the progress. The humor is that with most of the Association congregations were in Detroit A trip out to the wilds of what became Livonia on a paved Michigan "trunk line," Baseline Road, seemed a far trip. Don't forget, this was during the Great Depression. A small but significant historical footnote was that more than **40 years earlier, four west side Detroit churches had tried to establish their own Lutheran cemetery, but without success.**

The Board of Directors' Minutes of November 23rd, 1933, indicated some friction with **German Lutheran Cemetery**, as it had been known, the Cemetery of (Historic) Trinity Evangelical Lutheran Church and later known as Trinity Cemetery or Trinity Lutheran Cemetery. This cemetery – no longer owned by Trinity Congregation - is located on Mt. Elliott St. near the remnants of the old Packard Plant. The area is run-down, with many vacant lots from burned down old houses. Nevertheless the cemetery is in working order and not completely filled-up. Trinity Evangelical Lutheran Church is located near the downtown area of Detroit on Gratiot Ave. The cemetery is a few miles further north. Thankfully, the objection, which had to do with the advertising, was peacefully resolved.

The year of our Lord 1934, from an historical perspective, seemed to be a pivotal year in the United States and world. The country was still in the thick of the Great Depression, but unemployment decreased by 22%. Yet 1934 was arguably one of the worst years of the Great Depression as the world's economy hit rock bottom. As the global economic situation seemed hopeless, peoples and nations turned to whoever promised them a better life. At this time, the rising leaders used peoples' fears and prejudices to rally support and create a scapegoat for the world's problems. The year 1934 marked the rise of fascists and dictators.

However, 1934 was a further "development" year for Glen Eden Lutheran Memorial Park and the Lutheran Cemetery Association. The Board of Directors was increased from seven to nine members. More Lutheran churches were accepted into the LCA. The Lutheran Cemetery Association was still trying to reduce its indebtedness to the Glen Eden Development Co.

The roads in Glen Eden were graveled in 1935, but one can feel the tension in scores of Minutes between beautifying and improving the cemetery grounds and at the same time making owed payments. The Office of the LCA was now moved to the Lutheran Center Building, effective January 1st, 1936. Happily, attached to the Minutes of December 5th, 1935, was a specimen of the Glen Eden Memorial Association Certificate of Ownership of Glen Eden Lutheran Memorial Park, Livonia Township, Wayne County, Michigan, to various purchasers and the granting of sections in various blocks for burial ownership. Yet the LCA was still in arrears to the Glen Eden

Development Co. It was evident that the "founding fathers" were doing everything within their power to keep the cemetery from financial ruin. Monthly financial reports to the Board became more detailed, down to the penny, including repairs, stationery, postage, interest, light, and auto expenses. The LCA Board met 29 times in 1935!

The building of the "Tower of Peace" or Carillon Tower began in 1937. The maintenance barn was moved to the back of the Glen Eden property. No record is shown of the annual Memorial Service, but a curious notation on June 10th, 1937 stated: "Moved and carried that all music at (the) cemetery be played only by order of the Board." Humorously, was big band music introduced at Glen Eden and deemed inappropriate by pastors or Board members? We may never know! The Board also passed a resolution that no funerals be allowed at the cemetery on Sundays, Memorial Day, the 4th of July, Christmas, or New Year's Day.

Glen Eden Lutheran Memorial Park was slowly growing in strength and recognition, and in the very year (1937) that Detroit's own Joe Louis won the heavyweight boxing crown. At a second LCA (Annual!) Delegate meeting held in Advent of 1937, several addressed the group in laudatory words concerning Glen Eden and why still more interest should be shown in their Lutheran cemetery. **The Rev. F.A. Hertwig** – Pastor of Gethsemane, one of the most sacrificial of men and a strong proponent of Glen Eden - spoke on the vast difference of funerals as experienced by him in Glen Eden and that of a stock cemetery. Even during the era of the Great Depression, this was a time when Glen Eden's vision was to be *"The Most Beautiful Lutheran Cemetery in America."*

CB

Excursus – A "Glen Eden Story"

It was the era of the Great Depression. People did not have money; many were struggling to even keep their families housed and fed. Mr. Marty Moro shared a story about Glen Eden that touched his family. Mr. Moro, a Concordia University, Seward, Nebraska graduate and long-time LCMS Teacher, Development Officer at Concordia

University-Ann Arbor, and staff member at Lutheran Special Education Ministries, is now Executive Director of MOST (Mission Opportunities Short Term) Ministries. He tells us that his grandparents were members of Holy Cross Evangelical Lutheran Church in Detroit. Holy Cross was one of many Lutheran churches which were visited by Glen Eden salesmen to encourage parishioners – with the help of a supportive pastor – to purchase burial lots in Glen Eden Lutheran Memorial Park.

One of these parishioners was Mr. Moro's maternal grandfather, Walter R. Behnke. One day, during the Great Depression era, Mr. Behnke came home and told his wife, Ruth, that he had purchased graves at Glen Eden. Ruth was furious. Here they hardly had enough to live on, and dear Walter bought burial plots for them.

When Walter Behnke died in 1981, he was buried in the Garden of Hymns at Glen Eden Lutheran Memorial Park on January 13th, 1981. At that time, his wife, Ruth Behnke, learned that he had not bought just two plots but a section (four burial plots). She was angry at her late husband but later learned that her daughter and son-in-law (grandson Marty Moro's parents), had burial plots for them-selves, a very good thing! Apparently, she forgave her late husband. Ruth is buried next

to her husband, Walter Behnke, in the Garden of Hymns, being laid to rest 27 years later on Feb. 28th, 2008. Bravo to Walter for getting those plots, and at a cheap price, even during the Great Depression!

Right – The Garden of Hymns, with a monument of organ pipes.

Glen Eden Prior to the War Years

The latter years of the Great Depression saw the specter of war on the horizon in Europe and the Far East. Germany, Italy, and Japan had expansionist worldviews. Great Britain and France were standing together. The Soviet Union could not be trusted. The United States of America was maintaining an isolationist approach, wanting desperately to stay out of what seemed a likely world war.

Mr. Percival B. Warr continued to serve as General Manager of the Lutheran Cemetery Association. At the Annual LCA Delegate Meeting on February 4th, 1938, a rising vote of thanks was given to Mr. P.B. Warr as the General Manager of Glen Eden for his untiring labor in behalf of the cemetery. However, Mr. Warr's health gave out the next year, and he died just prior to the start of World War II and the German invasion of Poland. His grave is in the Brookside Garden of Glen Eden West. (See page 131.)

Grave blankets at Christmas were first noted in 1939. The first decade of Glen Eden Lutheran Memorial Park's existence came to an end in 1939. War would soon be raging across Europe. The United States would eventually be drawn into World War II. But for now, Detroit's auto industry was surging forward, and even with all the minutia of running and maintaining a cemetery, our Memorial Park was growing under the gracious hand of the Heavenly Father.

Left: Detroit from across the Detroit River in Windsor, Ontario, Canada. It is the only major American city having with an international border.

The Second Decade: A Time of World War, Missing Minutes, and Significant Change

Detroit was emerging out of the Great Depression in the late 1930's, though unemployment was still high at around 10%. However, the auto industry was booming, churches were growing in the city, and the population by 1940 in Detroit reached 1,623,452. It would peak after the 1950 census (1,849,568). During the years 1940 to 1950, the Black (African-American) population would more than double from 149,119 to 300,506. A deadly race riot would occur in June, 1943, in which 34 were killed, most black. Social tensions were heightened amid the military build-up of the participation of the United States in World War II. Detroit's auto industry would also convert to aid mightily in the war effort. Meanwhile, Glen Eden Memorial Park continued to grow.

At the February 2nd, 1940 LCA Delegate Meeting, Mr. Henry Martens, Board Chairman, and Rev. Herman Metzger presented separate historical overviews and word pictures of the progress of the cemetery. A Delinquents Committee was formed to get after the growing number (and amount) of delinquencies on burial plot payments. By early 1940, the following information was disclosed:

BURIAL RECORD

(Historical note: In 1930, there were two adult burials and one child burial, yet the Burial Record below records only two.)

1930 - - - - - - - - - 2	1941 - - - - - - - - - - 7
1931 - - - - - - - - - 9	(513)
1932 - - - - - - - - - 18	
1933 - - - - - - - - - 24	PASTOR'S POINT 15
1934 - - - - - - - - - 47	BLOCK #2 128
1935 - - - - - - - - - 39	BLOCK #11 238
1936 - - - - - - - - - 52	BLOCK #12 0
1937 - - - - - - - - - 68	BLOCK #13 31
1938 - - - - - - - - - 71	BLOCK #15 23
1939 - - - - - - - - - 73	BLOCK #17 28
1940 - - - - - - - - - 103	(513)

In the next decade, blocks would then take on the name "Gardens."

(Below, the Carillion Tower)

Grave marker of one of the "founding fathers" of the Lutheran Cemetery Association and long-time Board of Directors member and officer, the Rev. Herman Metzger (1879-1954) and his wife, Emma. They are buried in Pastor's Point in Glen Eden Lutheran Memorial Park West.

A touching historical footnote appeared in the Minutes of the LCA Delegate Meeting, held on October 4th. "Pastor (H.A.) Quitmeyer reported on the death of a poor brother Lutheran and thanked the Association for their part in furnishing a grave." Many such Christian charity activities were performed over the decades by Glen Eden, and only a few, such as this, were actually recorded.

This practice of Glen Eden giving charitable contributions to various organizations in the LCMS, WELS, and locally has shown Glen Eden Lutheran Memorial Park's desire to be involved with local charities and national, confessional Evangelical Lutheran colleges, universities, seminaries, and Michigan Lutheran high schools.

ɞ

Excursus - The Fackler Family's Dedication to Glen Eden

Almost since its inception, a few families have served generationally across the decades on the Board of Directors of the Lutheran Cemetery Association and Glen Eden Lutheran Memorial Parks. The graves of some of Fackler family members is a testimony of faithful and continuous service to the Lord God and His people associated with Glen Eden Memorial Parks.

The Rev. Ernest Carl Fackler was Pastor of St. Andrew Evangelical Lutheran Church, Detroit, from 1910 to 1951. He served on the LCA Board of Directors (during the years of the missing Minutes) and in giving sermons at Memorial Services and motivational talks at Annual Delegate meetings, and promoting the purchases of burial plots. He is buried in Pastor's Point. His grandson (the older brother of Mr. Ernest ["Ernie"] Carl Fackler III, current Board Chairman), died in his mother's

womb, a very touching story in itself. Ernest Carl Fackler III was born a year later, even though the doctor had warned the mother not to have any more children. Mr. E. Carl (Ernest C.) Fackler Jr. (Ernie's father) served 35 years on the Board of Directors, as the Secretary (1954-1976), then Vice Chairman (1976-1983), and finally Chairman of the Board of Directors (1983-1988). He and his wife, Emma, are buried in Garden of Prayer, as is their baby boy. Mr. Ernest ("Ernie") C. Fackler III has been serving on the Board of Directors for decades and as Board Chairman since 2019, having served previously as Vice Chairman (1995-2018). Ernie's wife, Karen, was laid to rest in the Fackler section of "God's acre" in 2020 in the Garden of Prayer.

☙

While sales were gradually increasing, the delinquent accounts amount rose to over $20,000 by August 14th, 1941. Yet the cemetery grounds continued to be expanded as to the opening of new blocks (later called "gardens"), purchases of fertilizer, outdoor maintenance and indoor office equipment, tiles, road paving, advertising in the Lutheran Center newspaper, the *Detroit Lutheran*, and attendance at national cemetery convention meetings. Improvement was also made in terms of prompt monthly payments from the LCA to the Glen Eden Development Co.

Nothing was recorded in Glen Eden's Board Minutes as to the December 7th Japanese bombing of the United States Navy at Pearl Harbor, Oahu, Hawaii, and the U.S. declaration of war against the Axis powers of Japan, Germany, and Italy. No doubt it was on the minds and hearts of the Board members. The United States would quickly be entering a new phase of war production that would greatly affect Detroit and the auto industry. But for Glen Eden, the biggest problem confronting the Board of Directors of the Lutheran Cemetery Association by this point in history seemed to be that of delinquent accounts. The number of delinquencies and growing amount was a major concern.

A Major Board Change in 1943 – Year of Crisis

In rapid succession, three Board of Directors members resigned in late 1942 and early 1943 due to a work schedule change (Mr. Charles J. Dallmann), ill-health (Board Chairman, Mr. Henry M. Martens), and a change of residence (Board Secretary, Mr. Henry C. Schatz) to Tawas City, MI,. This was the most momentous change in the Lutheran Cemetery Association's leadership in its dozen-plus years of existence. Appreciation for the gracious work of the three Lutheran Cemetery Association Board members was expressed, complete with a letter of thanks, sent to each of them.

Glen Eden Lutheran Memorial Park and the Lutheran Cemetery Association were at a very serious and critical junction. Financial difficulties and indebtedness had mounted. Of special historical note is the April Board Minutes is a report of Mr. Nordlie for the Finance Committee:

> He went into details as to the many sessions held between the committee members and two meetings with an attorney whom the committee interviewed with the thought of retaining counsel. He went into detail and stated that **on the basis of the financial statement for 1942 the Association could pay off nothing of its debt. A study of the finances over the past six years would indicate that the indebtedness to the Glen Eden Development Company and to Nelson Stuckey would have to be refunded if possible over a period of many years**, possibly forty, and that the total debit to these two creditors should be reduced to approximately $100,000. The Finance Committee was willing to tackle the big job of getting the big reductions in order to save the Association and note holder's investment(s). If it was not possible to work out the discounts and refunding, it would be necessary to go to the congregation members of the Association and tell them the picture and ask them what their wishes might be for a continuance of the Association. (bold emphasis – ed.)

In addition, with the country at war, there was a labor shortage at the cemetery. At the April 15th, 1943 Board meeting, the six Departments (or Committees) reported. **Mr. Elmer Engel**, who became the longest serving member of the Board of Directors, was appointed as a new Board member. Tragically, Board Minutes are missing after April 15th, 1943 to January 20th, 1949. One may wonder why Minutes were missing?

In the wider picture of history, financial accountings, writings, and/or minutes of the founding of nation-cities, countries, empires, business, educational, or religious organizations, historical information is often not recorded, lost, stolen, destroyed in fires, volcanoes (Pompey and Herculaneum, A.D. 79), or flooding (Zion Lutheran, Detroit, June, 2021). Sometimes records or minutes might disappear due to theft, misplacement, or carelessness. Whatever the case, Glen Eden Minutes are largely lacking between 1943 and 1949. We can be grateful to the Lord that as much history of Glen Eden is safely in hand in the volumes present and in financial reports over several decades, independent of the minutes. Even *Roberts Rules of Order* grants some latitude to the secretaries and takers of minutes on how much or little detail should be recorded. However, it is unfortunate when minutes are missing.

The name of Mr. Elmer W. Engel (a Chrysler Corp. executive) is long remembered by several veteran members of the current Board  **of Directors and Staff for his decades of faithful service, especially as Treasurer, to Glen Eden Lutheran Memorial Park. He and his wife, Dorothea, are buried in the Garden of Prayer.**

What difficulties and enormous challenges confronted Glen Eden Lutheran Memorial Park and the Lutheran Cemetery Association can only be surmised. The Great Depression and World War II, plus the delinquency accounts and insufficient sales took a huge toll on Glen Eden, the Lutheran Cemetery Association, and the Board members. Mr. Wallinger, an Accountant, issued a two-page letter, indicating that it was necessary to go to a fiscal year accounting for those "missing years" of 1943 through 1948. He indicated that it was necessary to "do good," that is, to not falsify anything or put the LCA in a position of jeopardy. He reviewed reports submitted to the federal state, and local governments and the Securities and Exchange Commission. Apparently, his audit proved good for Glen Eden, with nothing amiss.

The decade came to a close on a seemingly sour note. There was a dispute regarding projected figures based on sales. It did get resolved. God was still guiding the leadership of Glen Eden Lutheran Memorial Park, this remarkable plot of ground, "God's acre" on Baseline Road in Livonia, finally to be incorporated as a city in 1950.

Left: Garden marker (indicator) for the Garden of Forgiveness. The wooden posts were later replaced with black iron posts for the garden markers.

Below: The Holy Bible in the Garden of Hope.

"May God be gracious to us and bless us and make His face to shine upon us, that Your way may be known on earth, Your saving power among all nations. Let the peoples praise You, O God; let all the peoples praise You."
– Psalm 67:1-3

Chapter 2
Financial Security and New Development

Again, God be praised! Matters improved considerably. 1950 was the turn-around year. With a bold, new policy, sales of burial plots soared. This policy was the simple (expediency) of selling land to obtain cash for Glen Eden's needs. This aggressive policy continued until 1956.

Re-Naming

In mid-1950, the blocks were renamed as gardens. Within each Garden there were, of course, sections, and a section consisted of four burial plots. Glen Eden did not have mausoleums or columbariums at this stage in its history. New names were: follows:

Block 1	**GARDEN OF FAITH**	(formerly, Hope)
Block 2	**GARDEN OF REST**	(formerly, Tranquility)
Block 11	**GARDEN OF PRAYER**	
Block 12	**EVERGREEN GARDEN**	
Block 13	**SUNRISE GARDEN**	
Block 15	**BROOKSIDE GARDEN**	
Block 17	**GARDEN OF MEMORIES**	
Block 19	**GARDEN OF PEACE**	

PASTOR'S POINT had already been developed and named.

This was perhaps a more significant step forward in Glen Eden's maturity as a Christian cemetery than realized at the time. These names reflected the geographic layout of Glen Eden Lutheran Memorial Park. They were accessed on roads fanning out from the Carillion Tower, with its large Cross on the tower's front. The names also suggest a Christian virtue or deportment, encompassing a reflection on God's grace and abiding peace. Some of the above-named Gardens would, in time, be modified. Eventually, more blocks would be developed and converted over to named "gardens" such as

Gardens of the Holy Trinity, Ascension, Hymns, Good Shepherd, and Reformation. The move to named gardens also likely helped attract sales among Lutheran grave purchasers.

Necessity is the mother of invention," or so the expression goes. Glen Eden did not own a backhoe in the early 1950s. Graves had to be dug by hand. A few cemeteries with which the LCA Board was in correspondence extolled the Sherman Power Digger. Glen Eden also was in need of addressing problems with the lake and the drainage system. The topography on the western side of Glen Eden Memorial Park needed to be addressed to make for satisfactory run-off. Backhoes would henceforth be an important part of the operation and maintenance of the cemetery.

1952 and 1953

The Board began 1952 by congratulating itself on the purchase of the backhoe (grave digger) 18 months earlier. Publicity through the *Detroit Lutheran* continued to be effective. Payments to the perpetual care fund, as part of the agreement with the Glen Eden Development Co., continued, but now in larger amounts. Money management and investment was now a greater part of running Glen Eden. A new **Garden of Victory** was developed, featuring a victory circle as the feature and using 1st Corinthians (15), verses 54 & 55. Also being added to the Memorial Park was a **Garden of Eternal Love**, **Garden of Consolation**, and **Companion Garden and Babyland** (later renamed Garden of the Lambs). Various monuments were also being added to several of the gardens.

Happily, a net profit for the year of 1952 amounted to $64,037.48. Rev. Herman Metzger was given a vote of thanks for over two decades of services; he made an honorary member of the Board. God was blessing the growth of Glen Eden Lutheran Memorial Park, the Lutheran Cemetery Association, the churches, and the families who buried their loved ones in Glen Eden. The Lord God's name was also being faithfully invoked in both an opening and closing prayer at each Board and Annual Delegate meeting. Money received from pre-need markers was now also being invested in the LCMS Michigan District's Church Extension Fund.

Excursus - Glen Eden's Neighbors (Other Cemeteries)

It is important to bear in mind that Glen Eden Lutheran Memorial Park in Livonia, Michigan, also has neighbor cemeteries. Some are very old in the Detroit metro area; some are relatively new. Some are part of an amiable "competition," and some have been valued friends in the cause of cemetery advocacy.

In Livonia, there are several old "pioneer" cemeteries, usually much smaller in size. These include: **Livonia Cemetery**, Farmington Road near Five Mile Road; **Newburg(h) Cemetery**, Ann Arbor Trail; **Clarenceville Cemetery**, south side of Eight Mile Road, just east of Middlebelt Road; and **Union Cemetery**, Eight Mile Road, east of Haggerty Road, just west of I-275. The larger cemeteries, include: **Parkview Memorial Cemetery**, Six Mile Road just west of Farmington Road, founded 1926, featuring an impressive arch entryway, built during the 1930s as a U.S. government work project; **Mount Hope Memorial Gardens**, Middlebelt Road, 54 acres, founded, 1952; **Beth El Memorial Park** (Jewish), Six Mile Road, west of Middlebelt Road; and **Adat Shalom Memorial Park**, immediately next to Beth El, on Six Mile. There are also Memorial Gardens, some with ashes that are scattered: **Felician Sisters Memorial Garden** (Roman Catholic) at Madonna University, Schoolcraft and Newburgh Roads; **St. Andrew's Memorial Garden** (Episcopal), Hubbard Road, north of Five Mile Road; **St. Matthew's Memorial Garden** (Methodist), Six Mile Road, east of Merriman Road; and **St. Paul's Memorial Garden** (Presbyterian), Five Mile Road at Inkster Road.

These cemeteries and memorial parks are Glen Eden's neighbors in Livonia. There were also nearby neighboring cemeteries across Eight Mile Road in **Farmington and Farmington Hills.** These included: **Oakwood Cemetery and** the old **Quaker Burial Ground.**

There are also old, historic and "rival" cemeteries and memorial parks in southeastern Michigan that have come into prominence and have garnered some of the "market," so-to-speak, especially regarding military burials. These include: **Elmwood Cemetery**, Detroit (the oldest continuous operating non-denominational cemetery in Detroit, established in 1846); **Mt. Elliott Cemetery** (Roman Catholic), Detroit; **Forest Lawn Cemetery, Woodmere Cemetery, Woodlawn Cemetery**, and **Grand Lawn Cemetery**, Detroit; **Mt. Olivet Cemetery**, Detroit's largest cemetery with 300 acres, established, 1888); **Franklin Cemetery**, Franklin, MI (1827); **Michigan Memorial Park Cemetery**, Flat Rock, MI; and **Great Lakes National Cemetery, Holly, MI**, established, 2005. This latter cemetery, offering free military service burials, has reduced the number of new burials of most cemeteries in southeastern Michigan.

☙

Another new garden was added in 1953, **The Garden of the Holy Trinity**. Since there were term limits on the Board of Directors, the Board had to prepare itself to elect new members in 1954. But another new milestone was forthcoming: the liquidation of the debt to Lutheran Cemetery Association "note holders." The note holders would be paid a 5% liquidation dividend out of the General Fund. The cemetery was on stronger footing. This led to the desire of the Glen Eden Development Co. to be terminated, 18 months ahead of schedule. However, this request was tabled for action until the Board's July meeting. As at so many board meetings, approval was given for the adding of more trees to the Park.

At the February 1954 Annual (Delegate) Lutheran Cemetery Association meeting, each delegate received a copy of the maps of Glen Eden Lutheran Memorial Park, as well as an Annual Report. This may not seem like a big deal in our day, but it certainly was back in 1954. Pictures of the work done on the bridge and pictures of the Gardens was also passed around.

Meetings of the Board of Directors continued to be held in the evenings, usually beginning at 7:30 p.m. and often ending at or past 11:00 p.m. A resolution was introduced to limited meetings to two hours, but it was defeated! Delinquent accounts were reduced over the years. By March, 1954, delinquencies only amounted to $1,583. Long-time member, Rev. Herman Metzger, died in 1954; the Board gave a memorial in his memory. Due to Michigan legislation against a funeral director being involved with the management of a cemetery, Mr. Harry Will reluctantly had to resign from the Board of Directors.

America was also changing in the post-World War II years of the baby boom and younger American families purchasing homes in the growing suburbs. American cities were just starting to peak. Detroit had already hit its high-water mark in population in 1950, but the churches and ordinary citizens did not anticipate the changes that were to come, particularly with demographic changes and a growing African-American (Black) population. The Cold War was on, and the United States and her Allies (Canada, France, and Great Britain and their respective empires) stood against the Communist Soviet Union and mainland China and their allies. The nuclear era was still coming of age, and fear of Communism permeated the minds of Americans. But gas was cheap, and life was generally good.

Glen Eden Lutheran Memorial Park was becoming noted for its trees and shrubbery and Memorial Services at the Park. In the early 1950's, **Glen Eden had picnic grounds in the cemetery**, complete with tables. Sadly, the picnic grounds had to be discontinued for safety and other reasons, such as kids playing on graves and not showing proper respect! Very few cemeteries and memorial parks today have picnicking grounds and play areas.

At this time, the cemetery had road names for the various drives in the Park. The cost to change the names was prohibitive at that time, but apparently desired. At the June 6th, 1954 Annual Memorial Service, the Lutheran Choralaires and an Honor Guard from American Legion Post 406 performed. Various memorial gardens were now being completed.

The Lord Jesus said, *"Let not your hearts be troubled. Believe in God; believe also in Me. In My Father's house are many rooms* ("mansions" - KJV). ... *I am the way, and the truth, and the life. No one comes to the Father, except through Me."* - John 14:1-2, 6

Good Shepherd statue in the Garden of the Good Shepherd.

"The Lord is my Shepherd, I shall not want." (Psalm 23:1)

A hymn stanza: O Christ, the Good Shepherd, *"You are the Great High Priest; You have prepared the feast Of holy love; And in our mortal pain None calls on You in vain; Our plea do not distain; Help from above."* - Shepherd of Tender Youth (LSB 864:3)

At that same Annual Delegate Meeting of the Lutheran Cemetery Association on February 4th, 1955, a proposal for a complete revision of the Constitution and Bylaws of the Lutheran Cemetery Association in accord with the modern needs of the Association was approved. This revision would then be submitted for approval at the next annual meeting. This was significant. The old Lutheran Cemetery Association and its Constitution and Bylaws had served well for the purpose of developing a Lutheran cemetery, but a new organizational structure was needed for Glen Eden Lutheran Memorial Park. Also, another garden had now been added, **Garden of the Ascension.** But now would come something new.

An Ecclesiastical Corporation

The beginnings of a new corporation started in 1955, a new non-profit corporation, an ecclesiastical corporation. The reason for the proposed change in the corporate set-up was that the old LCA could not amend its Constitution so as to provide for the future development of the cemetery, the sale of bronze memorial markers, etc. The main purpose of amending the original articles was to circumvent legal action on the part of monument manufacturers and distributors who, in the past, had threatened to restrain Glen Eden from selling memorial bronze markers because the old charter did not so provide. If a new charter as an ecclesiastical corporation could be obtained, the cemetery association would be in a much better corporate position, among other things giving the benefit of exemption from payment of sales tax. The new charter would also permit Glen Eden to set forth her own purposes as opposed to attempting to amend them in the past corporation set up.

The Lutheran Cemetery Association Delegate body on April 28th, 1955, resolved to dissolve itself in favor of a new organization, still called the Lutheran Cemetery Association, but as an ecclesiastical corporation in which the Board of Directors would also have greater hands-on involvement in the cemetery. (Later on, this would come to be known as "Glen Eden Lutheran Church".)

Back to the cemetery, itself! The Memorial Service on Sunday, June 5th, 1955 featured sacred music from the Tower of Peace (Carillon Tower), considerable music by the Holy Cross Evangelical Lutheran Church Choir and a soloist, the singing of the hymn, *"I Know That My Redeemer Lives,"* the participation of three pastors, a Memorial Tribute by the Detroit Lutheran Post No. 406 of the American Legion, and the Placing of a Memorial Wreath by the Detroit Lutheran Gold Star Mothers. The tower was featured on the front cover of the Service folder. One could easily see the effects of the Second World War in terms of the emphases in the Memorial Service, which included the Memorial Address by the Rev. Armin W. Born, Pastor of Holy Cross Evangelical Lutheran Church.

A lot of careful detail was given to the gardens in Glen Eden, especially in adding new shrubbery, trees, and memorial items prior to the opening of a particular garden. Such dedication! Mr. Alvin Meyer was now serving, as of August 1st, 1955, what would be a long and blessed tenure as General Manager.

In 1956, Glen Eden finally reached the position for the first time in its history of owning the entire acreage that constitutes the memorial park – both (the) Glen Eden Development Co. and the Hitchman Land Contract were liquidated! Glen Eden Lutheran Memorial Park now possessed the deeds to all the land. Moreover, the indebtness to the noteholders was reduced a full 25%.

1956 was a momentous year in the United States of America and world. A recession had occurred in this year of the Eisenhower Administration, but the interstate highway system was inaugurated and began to be built. Singing sensation Elvis Presley appeared on the Ed Sullivan Show. American actress Grace Kelly married Prince Rainier III of Monaco. The Suez Canal crisis led to war between Egypt and Israel. The Soviet Union would soon enter the space age with their first Sputnik, causing increasing fears of spying and nuclear wars. The U.S.S.R. crushed the Hungarian Revolution with brut military power. Cecil B. de Mille's epic film, *The Ten Commandments,* was released. The Detroit Red Wings were hoping for back-to-back Stanley Cup titles, led by Gordie Howe. The auto industry was booming, and that was great for Detroit. The most popular car in 1956 was the iconic Chevrolet (Chevy) Corvette. Lutheran churches in the greater Detroit area and in the city were at their virtual height. Some of the suburbs, including Livonia and western Wayne County were growing rapidly.

The Issue of Race

As to race and ethnicity, America was changing. Even though the Civil War (1861-1865) and President Abraham Lincoln's Emancipation Proclamation freed the slaves in 1863, it would take a century for segregation and unfair practices toward those who were not Caucasians to be addressed through civil rights marches, legislation, and vast changes in schools, business, and voting rights for racial equity to be achieved. Progress was being made in the military during World War II and in baseball and other sports.

This issue was not new to this nation and continent. Dehumanizing actions that have been practiced from time immemorial were finally being significantly addressed in this nation in the 1950s and 1960s. Glen Eden was not exempt from cultural practices in vogue, even before the cemetery came under Lutheran auspices. It was, however, addressed by the Board, and a prior practice of exclusion from burial in Glen Eden Lutheran Memorial Park was altered. Today one easily notices that other races and ethnic groups and Christian denominations – including Asian, African-American, Middle Eastern, Orthodox, Roman Catholic, etc. – are buried in the Glen Eden cemeteries.

The monument of the Evangelists – Saints Matthew, Mark, Luke, and John – in the Garden of the Evangelists.

Further Development and Expansion, and a New Name

The Disastrous Fire

On May 25th, 1956, a major fire of undetermined origin destroyed the Service (Maintenance) building and its contents. Many of the bronze markers were ruined. Many of the items that were destroyed were then replaced. Thankfully, the insurance policy covered this equipment against theft, fire, vandalism, and accidents, but funds would still be needed for a new replacement building and for hiring an architect. The Board acted quickly; by 1957 a new Service Building was completed.

At this time, the Office building was directly fronting on Eight Mile (Baseline) Road, in Livonia, just west of the lake (pond), but a layout of the Glen Eden Memorial Park noted a future office just east of the lake, but west of the main entry road. This would, naturally, be changed when still another new office was built and dedicated in 1992.

Also at this time, a few smaller Lutheran cemeteries were being removed and relocated at Glen Eden Lutheran Memorial Park, including those of St. John Evangelical Lutheran Church, Rochester, MI, and Fraser Lutheran Church Cemetery, Fraser, MI.

Humor, Serious Discussion, and an Important Letter

At the LCA Annual Meeting held at Gethsemane Evangelical Lutheran School on February 8th, 1957, there was a humorous "official complaint" registered by the delegate from St. Stephen Evangelical Lutheran Church. His complaints were as follows:

1. A Glen Eden salesman with a masonic pin tried to sell property to him, which he resented.
2. The Office was not conducted in a business-like manner. **He found women smoking and very noisy** when he had to visit the office during a work day.

We can assume it was okay for the men to smoke, but 1957 was a different world than in this 21st century. Rev. MacKenzie, Board Chairman, had something else in his **Report to the LCA Annual Meeting** which is of startling and almost humorous significance. His Report stated what had caused years of confusion as to Glen Eden's existence:

> Our other outstanding accomplishment – again without glamour – is our **dissolution of the Glen Eden Memorial Association**. Most people are not acquainted with this particular organization. It preceded the Lutheran Cemetery Association in point of incorporation…. The Memorial Association was evidently established for the purpose of making profits from the proceeds of sales made by the Lutheran Cemetery Association. In sum and substance, after the last lot had been sold and all indebtedness retired, the Glen Eden Memorial Association would have assumed control and ownership. Profits would have been paid as dividends to all stockholders which included individuals, some not connected with the Lutheran Church at all, and some churches. **This Memorial Association would have gained control of the**

Perpetual Care Fund and would have been able to dissolve the fund and divide the assets among the stockholders thereby defeating the intent and purpose of our present Association – to provide a beautiful memorial park for the repose of bodies of our brothers and sisters in our holy faith until the glorious day of resurrection.

After much study of the problem,… we determined to seek dissolution of the corporation (i.e., the Glen Eden Memorial Association) through the Securities Commission of the State of Michigan. This could not have been done until the Glen Eden Development Co. had (been) dissolved. When this company passed out of the picture, we dissolve(d) the Glen Eden Memorial Association. This has been accomplished. On January 17, 1957 the Memorial Association ceased to exist. **Today the Lutheran Cemetery Association stands as the undisputed owner of every inch of the 174 acres of land dedicated as God's Acre** for the safe repose of our beloved.

Hence all stock certificates issued prior to Jan. 17 are now worthless save as souvenirs of a defunct corporation. They never had any value and so no individual and no church lost anything through possession of these certificates. In reality, this step has saved the Lutheran churches much grief, time, effort, money…

Your Board of Directors is happy… to make this report. **We are very conscious that God has used the talents He has given each of us** so that they goals have been achieved by Him through men who know that in whatever they do they must first serve Him! (bold highlights – ed.)

One wishes one could have been a fly on the wall that night of the Annual Meeting in early February, 1957. Certainly, from an historical perspective, a huge debt of gratitude is owed to the Board of Directors.

Now on the horizon was the possibility of purchasing **additional land of the Henry Evert Farm, 79 acres on the north side of Eight Mile Road in Farmington Hills, Oakland County.** This property would bring the acreage of Glen Eden Lutheran Memorial Park to 253 acres.

However, the Evert family continued to lease the farm for the next year. Meanwhile, the tower was decorated for the Christmas season, with Christmas music being played throughout the cemetery every afternoon.

Excursus – Glen Eden Lutheran Church

St. Patrick's Day, March 17th, 1959, saw a very important Board of Directors' meeting. **There was a Charter problem**. The Michigan Corporation and Securities Commission had turned down the renewal of the Charter. A proposal to incorporate under an ecclesiastical corporation had been turned down by three Association churches. The Board then decided to organize as a Lutheran Church Corporation to take over the cemetery and provide for possible services. A name suggested was Resurrection or Church of the Resurrection, though the cemetery would be run in its regular manner. **The name, however, would ultimately be "Glen Eden Lutheran Church,"** a Michigan Ecclesiastical Corporation.

Glen Eden Lutheran Church as an imaginary church building (left), a non-synodical Lutheran church, not as a building, but as an ecclesiastical corporation. This would provide security for Glen Eden Memorial Park and Memorial Parks for decades to come. In the Year of our Lord 2023, Glen Eden is legally a 501c13, not a 501c3, as an ecclesiastical corporation since 1959, existing for the purpose of cemetery or burial activities, a Perpetual Care Fund (memorial parks, columbarium, etc.). This was reaffirmed by the State of Michigan in 1989. Hence the official name of the corporation is Glen Eden Lutheran Church, with a secondary

name of Glen Eden Lutheran Memorial Park, today now known as Glen Eden Lutheran Memorial Parks.

Why is this so significant? The Glen Eden Lutheran Church, while not a church as such, has and does provide for Memorial Services by the pastors on the Board of Directors (or other pastors of congregations of the Lutheran Cemetery Association, that is, of the churches of the synods that comprised the Evangelical Lutheran Synodical Conference of North America.) While the "Synodical Conference" today no longer exists, the constituent synods – the Missouri and Wisconsin Synods - constitute the Board of Directors as well as the Glen Eden Lutheran Memorial Parks Association. The LCMS and WELS uphold the confessional writings of the Evangelical Lutheran Church of 1580 or Book of Concord ("Concordia") with a full confessional subscription. The Confessions are in all their parts in full agreement with the Word of God (Holy Bible).

Moreover, without the annual, quarterly, or occasional Memorial Services, the 1959 Articles of Association would not be apparent. **The Memorial Services are constitutive to the existence of Glen Eden.** They are conducted in the Chapels or on the grounds of Glen Eden Memorial Parks. The Chapel at Glen Eden Memorial Park West in Livonia is the Mausoleum Chapel of Memories and the Chapel at Glen Eden Memorial Park East in Macomb is the actual Memorial Chapel itself.

"The steadfast love of the Lord never ceases; His mercies never come to an end; they are new every morning; great is Your faithfulness." Lamentations 3:22-23

Grave marker of Arthur & Josephine Ude, buried in the Garden of the Good Shepherd. Mr. Ude, a faithful servant of the Lord, was the attorney for Glen Eden. "It is a matter of record that Mr. Ude lived and breathed Glen Eden. There was no phase of cemetery operation in which he was not interested."

In late 1959, Mr. Wm. Campau was appointed Acting Grounds Superintendent until General Manager Meyer indicated otherwise. Mr. Carl Thompson had now taken over Glen Eden's legal files from the late Arthur Ude's office. Interments for 1959 were the highest ever per year at 398. No Board meeting was held in December; instead, the Board got together for a Christmas Dinner at Creger's Pickwick (German) Restaurant, thus beginning a pleasant annual tradition for the Board of Directors and their spouses.

The current roadway bridge over the creek flowing from the lake (pond) at Glen Eden Memorial Park West.

Chapter 3

Glen Eden during nationally tumultuous Years – The 1960's-mid-1970's

Glen Eden Memorial Park boldly moved forward into the next decade, the decade of the 1960's, unaware of the country entering into a most difficult period in the history of the United States of America. The 1960's also saw the fear of a nuclear holocaust intensify as the "Cold War" with the Soviet Union, the Warsaw Pact, and Communist China and her allies continued to heat up. Nearby Cuba would become communist under Fidel Castro, leading to the Bay of Pigs (Cuba) and Missile Crisis in the early 1960's. American schools held regular air raid drills. The Civil Rights Movement, the increasing U.S. involvement in what became an unpopular Vietnam War, the rise of the hippies, free sex, anti-war, and drug culture all began affecting American life, thinking, and norms, and the Church's role in society.

The '60's were also marred by the assassinations of President John F. Kennedy (1963), Civil Rights leader Dr. Martin Luther King, Jr.(1968), and Presidential candidate Robert Kennedy (1968). A strange response emerged inside and outside of the Christian Church in North America, the so-called "Jesus Revolution" or "Jesus Movement," which captured the hearts of many young people who wanted to embrace Christ while repudiating traditional Christianity and Christian congregations. Also, the news media became more and more prominent with Walter Cronkite of CBS and Chet Huntley & David Brinkley of NBC. The decade closed with the dramatic NASA Moon Landing in 1969.

The Evangelical Lutheran Synodical Conference of North America

Within North American Lutheranism, the "urge to merge" saw the creations of two major new Lutheran church bodies: **the new ALC** (American Lutheran Church, a merger of the old American Lutheran Church of 1930, the [Norwegian] Evangelical Lutheran Church, the LCF [Lutheran Free Church] and UELC [Danish United Evangelical Lutheran Church, called the "holy Danes"]), and **the LCA** (Lutheran Church in America, a merger in 1962 of the ULCA [United Lutheran Church in America], the Suomi Synod [Finnish], the AELC [Danish American Evangelical Lutheran Church, called the "happy Danes"], and the Augustana [Swedish] Synod (later in 1963). The member synods of the Evangelical Lutheran Synodical Conference of North America were not in pulpit-altar fellowship with the ALC and larger LCA. However, **higher biblical criticism, which denies the infallibility and authority of God's holy Word,** was creeping into the Lutheran Church—Missouri Synod at her Concordia Seminary, St. Louis; Concordia Senior College, Fort Wayne, IN; and various Concordia colleges and universities, especially at Bronxville, NY, and River Forest, IL. The *"battle for the Bible"* was on.

This latter development in the LCMS affected Glen Eden and the Lutheran Cemetery Association. While only the churches of the Wisconsin and Missouri Synods were part of the Lutheran Cemetery Association, the WELS and ELS (Evangelical Lutheran Synod) left the Synodical Conference in 1963 over the Missouri Synod's continued doctrinal slide toward theological liberalism. This tension was felt in the congregations of the greater Detroit area that were part of the Glen Eden Lutheran Cemetery Association. Tension arose between the WELS and LCMS pastors and congregations, and within the Missouri Synod as some pastors, such as LCA Board of Directors Chairman Rev. Cameron MacKenzie, felt the need to split from the LCMS and form a micro-synod. Most LCMS pastors and congregations stayed within the Missouri Synod during the 1960's, but tensions continued to grow.

Remarkably, Glen Eden Lutheran Church, as an ecclesiastical corporation, managed to survive during this very troublesome time within North American Lutheranism. The Lutheran pastors and congregations that did not leave the LCMS in the 1970's during the so-called "Seminex era" retained Lutheran confessional loyalty and cordiality with the "Glen Eden family," even if there were some tensions. The few congregations and pastors associated with the Lutheran Cemetery Association that aligned with the liberal ALC and LCA, ultimately left the LCMS and Glen Eden. They eventually merged in 1988, including the Missouri Synod's break-off, the AELC (Association of Evangelical Lutheran Churches), to form the ELCA Evangelical Lutheran Church in America). The ELCA is now even more outside the pale of confessional Lutheranism than in 1988.

It had been hoped that on Pentecost Sunday, June 5th, 1960, the new office building would be dedicated. However, delays postponed the building's completion to the Fall of 1960. The Evert Farm was also purchased outright by late Fall, using funds from the Perpetual Care Fund, which would be repaid.

The highlight of 1960 was the Dedication of the "new" Office Building on November 13th, 1960. It was followed by an Open House on January 14th, 1961, and the Annual Meeting of Glen Eden Lutheran Church as the cemetery's corporation was held on March 10th, 1961 at the Glen Eden Lutheran Memorial Park site.

The "new" office building by the lake (pond), pictured below.

A false report in the *Detroit Free Press* claimed that Glen Eden cemetery was operating incorrectly. This was totally incorrect! The newspaper article finally did get it right, acknowledging that the Michigan Corporation and Securities Commission stated that both Glen Eden and Woodmere cemeteries had filed annual corporate reports. Noteworthy in the article was the statement that Glen Eden Lutheran Church, Inc., was formed as an ecclesiastical corporation to "acquire, own, and operate Lutheran cemeteries," including the property formerly controlled by the association (i.e., Glen Eden Memorial Association). As an ecclesiastical corporation it was not required to file special perpetual care reports.

In effect, the *Detroit Free Press* had to eat crow, having not properly researched the matter. Nothing further was noted as to the articles in the *Detroit Free Press*. However, the Board was now giving consideration to a proposed Chapel and engaging an architect.

As an historical footnote, it should be remembered that Glen Eden Development Co. relinquished control in good faith. At times, the Company was in a position to resume control of the property and eliminate the Lutheran Cemetery Association completely. It did not choose to do so. Rather, it helped the Lutheran Cemetery Association reorganize and continue to purchase the property.

In the 1960's, efforts were made to save the Park's elm trees by spraying semi-annually against the Dutch Elm disease. During the same years, the owner and president of the Horner Wollen Mills, Mr. William Horner, had died, and that his estate had 500 sections, which was then re-purchased. This was important; the cemetery now had 2,000 more available graves. During these years, members of the Board of Directors continued to receive training in cemetery management from the American Cemetery Institute, located on the campus of Michigan State University, East Lansing.

The June 3rd, 1962 Annual Glen Eden Memorial Day Observance featured the Dedication and Unveiling of a new Veterans' Memorial Plaque and Monument in the Garden of Valor. It paid homage to the 318 Detroit area Lutherans who had given their lives in World War II and the Korean War (Conflict).

Right and on next page: Pictured is the Veterans Memorial Plaque and Monument, with 40-foot flagpole in the Garden of Valor (near the front entrance to Glen Eden West)

The June 3rd, 1962 Annual Memorial Day Observance, featuring the dedication of the Veterans Monument, was very well attended.

In 1962, Wayne County carried out its program of annexing 2,900 feet in length and 27 feet width, along Eight Mile Road frontage (southern portion) of our cemetery. A settlement was reached giving Glen Eden $10,655.00, but at a loss of 1,456 potential grave sites. Oakland County offered $5,000 for their northside portion of land.

The total acreage of the Memorial Park was 246 acres, 170 acres in Livonia in Wayne County and 76 acres in Farmington Hills in Oakland County, across from each other on Baseline (Eight Mile) Road. The Board at this time rejected offers for the Farmington Hills property.

Approximately a thousand people attended the Memorial Service at Glen Eden Memorial Park on June 2nd, 1963. During the year, further monuments were being designed and purchased from Rock of Ages in Barre, Vermont. Ice skating at the Park was a topic of consideration in

1963, but on the advice of the Glen Eden Attorney and the City of Livonia Legal Counsel, the Board decided against allowing such ice skating on the lake. Nor would the city of Livonia be policing or be responsible for any accidents from ice skating. The general rules of Glen Eden Lutheran Memorial Park also prohibited dogs, bicycling, and alcoholic beverages in the cemetery. Nevertheless, 1963 was regarded as a successful year for the Park, with 490 interments and a staff of eight grounds personnel maintaining 130 acres of the Park. However, guesstimates looked at exceeding 750 interments by the 1970's. Forty years later this would stabilize at around 700. The Perpetual Care Fund now stood at $293,805.09 in investments by the end of 1963.

Glen Eden's new Constitution had been re-written by Glen Eden's new Attorney, Mr. Carl Thomsen (later also Board Chairman). It was first read at the February 18th, 1964 Board of Directors' meeting and with a second reading six days later. The new Constitution and Bylaws were read at the March 6th, 1964 Annual Meeting. No action was taken since there were questions about Glen Eden's "purpose."

The Planning Committee of Glen Eden Board of Directors was now giving serious study to having a Chapel in Glen Eden Lutheran Memorial Park. What likely was not envisioned in the 1960's was the huge changes in America in terms of burial practices, including the rise of national cemeteries (free for any who served in the military), the huge rise in cremations and use of urns or no committals at all. This is not even to mention our 21st century national lack of understanding concerning the sanctity of human life and the importance that the Lord God places on human bodies that He created and which were temples of the Holy Spirit. But part of 1964's extraordinary news, though, was that General Manager Alvin Meyer had been elected to the presidency of the Greater Metropolitan Cemetery Association of Detroit, a distinct honor.

"Satisfy us in the morning with Your steadfast love, that we may rejoice and be glad all our days." - Psalm 90:14

Did the Board always rule?

One might get that impression. However, a most interesting thing happened in 1965 when the Board wanted to move from being Glen Eden Lutheran Church, an ecclesiastical corporation, to a lot-owners' association. At an Annual Meeting of Glen Eden Lutheran Church (of Glen Eden Lutheran Memorial Park) on May 14th, 1965, the assembly listened to a presentation by the Chairman, Rev. Cameron MacKenzie, and more extensive presentation by Attorney Carl Thomsen, Glen Eden's legal counsel. The assembly then took up the pros and cons of the type of corporation and ways of operating. The vote was then taken and the motion to scrap "Glen Eden Lutheran Church" was rejected! Here was a unique instance of the Association of Glen Eden Lutheran Church as an ecclesiastical corporation both retaining its legal entity name and rejecting the Board of Directors' recommendation. The delegates did not see the necessity of changing from Glen Eden Lutheran Church as an ecclesiastical corporation and may have also felt uneasy with a lot owners corporation, with the churches no longer being involved.

A big hubbub came about in mid to late 1965 concerning the Board's policy that only fresh-cut flowers could be placed on   graves from May 15th through September 30th. There was a strong push – in letters and by a huge petition with signatures – to "bring back artificial flowers." Guess what. Artificial (silk) flowers are permitted, as noted on the "Rules and Regulations" plaque at the entrance to the cemetery! **General Manager Alvin C. Meyer** (pictured left) was honored at the 1966 Annual Delegate Meeting. He served in that very important position from 1955 to 1984. Concurrently, **Mr. Elmer Engel** was still serving on the Board of Directors, having begun in 1943, and continuing till his death in 1996.

1967 brought the big news that in consultations for a Chapel-Mausoleum, **there was a growing national desire for above-ground entombments**. It was noted that a Chapel could be used for indoor crypt entombments and outdoor burials, especially in inclement weather. Building a Chapel-Mausoleum would come, but would indeed be a very expensive proposition.

Glen Eden's 79 acres - formerly the Evert Farm - on the northside of Baseline Road, was still farmed by Mr. Evert. However, he moved away in 1967 and was no longer caring for the property. This would now be Glen Eden's responsibility. In addition, the "well" on the Glen Eden property south of Eight Mile Road had gone sour. An analysis of it was being made by a Michigan state agency. With some effort and money, it got "sweetened" up.

The Ascension monument (pictured right) in the Garden of the Ascension, added in 1967

The Detroit Race Riots of 1967

Tensions were high in Detroit. Racial injustice was boiling over in numerous cities throughout America in the 1960s. The predominantly black (African-American) area of Virginia Park in Detroit was itself a seething caldron of racial tension. People lived in cramped neighborhoods and subdivided houses and apartments. The Detroit Police Dept. was viewed by African-Americans as highly discriminatory against them. In the Summer of 1967, cities where there were similar racial tensions erupted in violence, looting, rioting, and deaths.

Then, on Saturday night, July 22nd, and morning of the 23rd violence erupted in Detroit along 12th St., with looting soon following. Shops and businesses were ransacked, and then fires broke out that soon consumed the whole block. All city police and firefighters were called in. Detroit Mayor Jerome Cavanaugh asked Governor George Romney to send in the state police, but they could not control the angry, growing crowd. The National Guard was then called in. With snipers reportedly firing at firefighters and fire hoses being cut, Governor Romney then asked President Lyndon B. Johnson to send in U.S. troops. More than 7,000 people were arrested during the four days of rioting. A total of 43 people were killed, 1,700 stores had been looted. Nearly 1,400 buildings were burned. The "white flight" that had already begun in Detroit a decade earlier now became an avalanche of people leaving the city for good. Detroit lost much of its tax base. It was not until Detroit had slid from over 1.8 million people in 1960 to less than 650,000 in 2020 that the city slowly started a long trek back to improvement. While the economy of Detroit is today in 2023 stronger and "coming back," with parts of the city being revitalized, especially in the downtown and adjacent corridors, Detroit is a still a shadow of what it used to be.

Detroit Sports and the 1968 Detroit Tigers

The old English "**D**" became part of Detroit sports legend in the early 1880's with the Detroit Wolverines. Today it is associated worldwide with the Detroit Tigers as their symbol.

Detroit is home to four professional U.S. sports teams. It is only one of 12 cities to have four major North American sports. It is only one of four U.S. cities to have its MLB (Tigers), NFL (Lions), NHL (Red Wings), and NBA (Pistons) teams play within the city limits and the only American city to have its four teams play within its downtown area. The Red Wings during the golden years of Mr. Hockey, the late Gordie Howe, won 11 titles (Stanley Cups). A new Gordie Howe International Bridge is under construction between Detroit and her "southern" neighbor, Windsor, Ontario, Canada. While the Lions have never won a Super Bowl, even with the great Barry Sanders, they're being to roar and are an NFL play-off contender. The Pistons are another story.

The Tigers, though, played World Series games in 2006 and 2012 at Comerica Park. Gone are the days of old, beloved Tiger Stadium at Trumbull and Michigan Aves.(below) and the heroics of Ty Cobb and Hank Greenberg. Old Tiger Stadium (**below**) was badly out-of-date

and was in serious need of parking. **In 1968, "the year of the pitcher" in the Major Leagues, the Tigers won it all!** It was a team of superstars with career years, led by pitcher Denny McLain, who went 31-6 with a 1.96 ERA. The 1968 Tigers had a 113-win baseball season.

This was a helpful boost for Detroit, having just come through the horrific riots of 1967, which decimated part of the city. One can be sure that the 1968 Tigers were being talked about by Glen Eden Board members and staff with great joy.

Chapter 4

The Years Following the Detroit Riots

People change over the course of time. We are not immune from the world around us, and in leadership positions it is not uncommon for personalities to change. Other than anecdotal information, colored by the passage of time, we may not know how the personalities of those who shaped the history of Glen Eden Lutheran Memorial Park may have changed. All humans have foibles. But even apart from monumental events in human history, we all have egos, weaknesses, peculiarities, gifts, and abilities. The emphasis here is on the extreme dedication of many key individuals and others, often not named, who helped in making Glen Eden one of the most beautiful Lutheran cemeteries in America.

The nation, at this time of the late 1960's, was deeply divided by the unpopular war in Vietnam, where thousands of American servicemen were captured, wounded, or killed. Many felt it an unjust war. American soldiers returning from the war were shamefully mistreated or ignored, with little thanks for their heroic efforts. Moral bankruptcy and upheaval, amid the growing use of hallucinogenic drugs were further ripping apart American society. The Christian Church – catholic, holy, and apostolic – was also being affected by these fast and vast changes in society and culture. While the Civil Rights movement was continuing to gain momentum, metro Detroit was still reeling from the Detroit race riots of 1967, which would send the city into decades of "white flight," huge population loss, poverty, and lawlessness. The farther suburbs continued to grow as people left the city and the close-in suburbs.

However, Glen Eden Lutheran Memorial Park entered the year of 1969 on a strong note of continued growth. There were 669 total burials in 1968, 13 being Vietnam War casualties. Total assets at the end of 1968 finally stood at $1,299,794.58. 1969 appeared to be a quiet year for Glen Eden against the backdrop of decline in Detroit and violence and anger in the nation. The good news for Glen Eden was that by 1969 there were no more gravel roads in the Park. The total length of asphalt roadways in the cemetery was now 4.5 miles.

At the March 5th, 1971 Annual Meeting of Glen Eden Lutheran Church, General Manager Alvin Meyer shared with the delegates the plans for the Chapel and Mausoleum. Approval was given to proceed. Of special note was that **Mr. Alvin Meyer** was elected as President of the American Cemetery Association in 1973, an honor for him and Glen Eden, and that by this single honor he would really become "**Mr. Cemetery of the U.S.A.**" Meyer also projected that if Glen Eden reached 1,000 burials per year – possibly 86 more years could be projected. This represents an interesting projection, not including at this point a second and third Glen Eden East and St. Clair (County), the rapid increase decades later of cremations and columbariums, and other changes effecting cemeteries in southeastern Michigan such as the new National Cemetery in Holly, MI, for military veterans and spouses.

Annual Meetings, upon their completion of business and closing prayer during these years, resulted in the delegates, including pastors and guests, making an annual trek over to Huck's Bavarian Village Restaurant at Five Mile and Inkster.

Sadly, cemeteries are subject to vandalism. This happened a number of times in Glen Eden Lutheran Memorial Park's history in Livonia. In 1972, some bronze vases were stolen from graves. The hours of the watchman were from 4:30 to 9:00 p.m. Ads were placed by Glen Eden Lutheran Memorial Park in the local papers for return of the stolen items to police departments in the area. The theft struck a deep pathos of concern with the Board. How could a major theft occur at "our beloved cemetery"? As it turned out, 270 bronze vases were stolen, and the replacement cost was $8.00 per vase. The theft occupied the attention of the next several Board meetings. Solution. It was agreed to purchase an 840-foot-long chain-link fence and a 48-foot gate.

In 1972, at a regular Board of Directors' meeting, Chairman MacKenzie presented **a gift from Glen Eden to Mr. Alvin Meyer, General Manager**, as a token of esteem for his election to the presidency of the American Cemetery Association at San Francisco in August. It was a nice quartz watch. Still more good news for the year was that the building permit for the new Mausoleum was received in September, 1972. **The phase one construction of the Mausoleum-Chapel was completed, with a Dedication on June 2nd, 1974.** In 1975, the Annual Meeting was held in the Chapel.

1973 was a year of the "changing of the guard," so-to-speak. New officers were elected; others, like Attorney Mr. Carl Thomsen, became the new President (Chairman) and Pastor Cameron MacKenzie became the Vice Chairman. All of those who had served received "thank you" letters of appreciation from the Board of Directors for their service. Rev. MacKenzie would live only two more years. The best historical footnote to the end of this era are the words of English poet Alfred, Lord Tennyson (1809-1892) in *Morte d'Arthur* (the Death of [King] Arthur):

"The old order changeth, yielding place to new;
And God fulfills Himself in many ways, Lest one
good custom should corrupt the world."

The graves of long-term Chairman of the Board of Directors, Rev. Cameron A. MacKenzie, and his wife, Betty, are in Pastor's Point in Glen Eden Lutheran Memorial Park West. He died in the Lord in 1975. She died in the Lord in 1999.

The vast majority of Board meetings had been held at St. Matthew Evangelical Lutheran Church's Fellowship Hall in Detroit, where Rev. MacKenzie had served as Pastor and Glen Eden Board Chairman.

Now the Board of Directors held many of its regular meetings at Topinka's Country House at Seven Mile Road and Telegraph. In the United States, gasoline and other petroleum product prices were soaring during the 1973-1974 Oil Embargo. How did this affect Glen Eden Lutheran Memorial Park? As indicated by the General Manager, road repairs had to be delayed because asphalt and other petroleum products needed were in short supply. This affected the construction of the Mausoleum-Chapel, which finally did get completed in 1974.

✠ ✠ ✠

From 1969, with the election of the Rev. Dr. J.A.O. (Jack) Preus as president of The Lutheran Church—Missouri Synod, till the late 1970's, the LCMS would endure huge theological tensions resulting in a rift or "split," as noted earlier. These were troublous times, and one looks with discernment on how that crisis – sometimes referred to as the "Seminex" era and "the Battle for the Bible" affected so many. The conservative Missouri Synod retained its overall confession. The "working together" relationship between the LCMS and WELS on Glen Eden's Board of Directors and the Annual Meetings calmly continued. Rev. Victor Halboth, Jr., was as elected to the Board in 1975, beginning a 30-year span of service, 26 years of which were as Chairman of the Board. He was involved with the efforts keep the English District united and remaining in the Missouri Synod.

However, Glen Eden Lutheran Memorial Park was enjoying a season of real growth and progress. **The Garden of Victory** still was lacking a monument feature but in 1977 a striking monument (next page) was built. The engraved words on the monument are St. Paul's Divinely-inspired words from the Great Resurrection Chapter of the Holy Bible, I Corinthians, Chapter 15.

"O death, where in thy sting? O grave, where is thy victory? The sting of death is sin; and the strength of sin is the law. But thanks be to God, who gives us the victory through our Lord Jesus Christ." – I Corinthians 15:55-57

Chapter 5
The Late 1970's & 1980's: Moving in a Different Direction

In serving families, **Burial Interments, Entombments, and Inurnments** ranged from 679 in 1968 to 764 in 1978, with the highest number in those years being 815 in 1971. In other words, there appeared a growing consistency of numbers.

The pond and fountain closest to the Mausoleum-Chapel, below. Picture taken from near the Pump House. All of the ducks and ducklings took off when the photographer drew nigh!

In the late 1970's, Glen Eden's undeveloped property, particularly that of the Farmington Hills parcel (former Evert Farm), was under investigation for possible taxation. Local, state, and federal governments were all eager for more tax revenue. Farmington Hills began taxing Glen Eden, even though it was a non-profit ecclesiastical corporation. Glen Eden had desired to eventually develop the property as part of the cemetery in Oakland County but because it had not been platted for development, it became fair game for taxation. The decade of the 1970's came to a close for Glen Eden Lutheran Memorial Park. After years of legal wranglings and appeals, the Board in 1986 made the decision to sell the property north of Eight Mile Road, but that also would take years to finally culminate in a sale.

ദ

Excursus – The Backbone of Glen Eden – The Faithful Maintenance Crew

The Lord God has blessed Glen Eden Lutheran Memorial Parks with dedicated, devoted men in the cemetery's maintenance department. What is amazing is the incredible longevity of service of many of these workers. Currently in 2023, **Mr. Maurice Cupp**, for example, has over 40 years in service at Glen Eden West, part-time, and then full-time since 1984. The stories he can tell are amazing. He and current Grounds Superintendent, Mr. Greg West, will joke about how the Garden Chapel, which was added later in phase three of the Mausoleum-Chapel building program, is the "heat box." In Summer, that section of the Mausoleum catches the direct rays of the sun and becomes intensely hot. They also explained things as to the faceted glass windows in the Mausoleum, both the original exterior ones and the interior ones, added later and seen in both chapels but from opposite sides. Did you know, for instance, that when the Mausoleum was finally completed in all three phases of construction over the course of 20-plus years that in an aerial view it has the shape of a Cross?

Rarely can one catch all of the workers together, even at their designated break time. If they are involved in a particular maintenance project, one or a couple of them may want to finish it first before taking a break. One can only appreciate the hard work of these men during inclement weather and during days of extreme heat or cold. Yet taking care of the needs of our families is a hallmark of their dedication to duty and care.

Maybe you have noticed that Glen Eden has welcomed a staff that is often "family," not just a family of those who work together, but also of generations within a family, whether on the Board of Directors, Office Staff, or the Maintenance Crew.

**Left: Maurice Cupp & Matt Fulkerson are pictured with "Leroi."
This compressor, still in use, was built in 1953 by the Leroi Mfg. Co. of Milwaukee and acquired in 1966.
Right: Two backhoes in the Maintenance (Service) Bldg. at the back of the cemetery. Matt is sitting in the cab of the big backhoe. Standing in front are Terry & Maurice Cupp.**

Glen Eden has been truly blessed by a high level of service and dedication. In short, these servants regard Glen Eden as "home." Glen Eden "farms out" the grass cutting at both the Glen Eden West and East cemeteries under contract to Apartment Services, a firm run by a father and son, George & Mike La Forest. They have done a good job over the course of decades. Their company cuts over 90 cemeteries' lawns from Michigan to Pennsylvania.

"Oh, magnify the Lord with me, and let us exalt His name together." – Psalm 34:3

If the 1970's were to some degree an extension of the chaos and cultural upheavals of the 1960's, the 1980's were different. The Vietnam War was a thing of the past. More conservative political leaders emerged with great influence, Margaret Thatcher (Prime

Minister) in Great Britain and Ronald Reagan (President) in the United States. Free market economies were fueled by socio-economic changes due to advances in technology and worldwide free-wheeling laissez-faire capitalism; these stood in stark contrast to the stagnation of the 1970's. The AIDS-HIV epidemic was now recognized as a global threat to individuals and nations. Many U.S. corporations were moving their factories to Mexico, South Korea, Taiwan, China, and Thailand. This would affect Detroit and the auto industry. Global warming alarms were being sounded in political and scientific communities, in academia, industry, and nations.

The final decade of the Cold War opened with the United States-Soviet confrontation fully engaged, with no end in sight. Super-power tensions escalated rapidly as President Reagan scrapped the policy of détente and adopted a new, much more aggressive stance toward the Soviet Union and its Warsaw Pact allies. The fall of the Berlin Wall in 1989 was the herald of the imminent collapse of Soviet communism.

805 interments occurred in Glen Eden Lutheran Memorial Park in 1983, each representing a deceased person, with a mourning family who would find comfort in the Lord at Glen Eden. With the first addition to the Mausoleum, 360 crypts and 686 niches for cremations were now ready for purchase since the addition was completed in May, 1983 (Dedication in 1985).

The great variety of trees has made Glen Eden Lutheran Memorial Park a place of beauty, tranquility, and peace in remembering the faithful departed.

The blessed man: "He is like a tree planted by streams of water that yields its fruit in its season, and its leaf does not wither."
- Psalm 1:3

The Annual Meeting of Glen Eden Lutheran Church was held on February 22nd, 1985 at Topinka's Country House, with 34 delegates present. **Mr. Alvin Meyer had retired as General Manager after 29 years faithful service and was so recognized.** Mr. Richard Press, a Board member, was introduced to the delegates as the new General Manager. It was noted, amusingly, that Treasurer Franklin Schmidt did a commercial for the Detroit Tigers. The delegates were informed that the Dedication of the new wing (Phase II addition) of the Mausoleum would occur in October. That Dedication did take place on November 10th, 1985.

A Prayer of Moses, the man of God. *"Lord, You have been our dwelling place in all generations. Before the mountains were brought forth, or ever You had formed the earth and the world, from everlasting to everlasting, You are God."* - Psalm 90:1-2

The Sale of the Farmington Hills Property and the Start of the Glen Eden Enhancement Project

As mentioned, 1986 marked the beginning of the effort to sell Glen Eden Lutheran Memorial Park's Farmington Hills property. It would take six years to accomplish this. It is almost a saga in itself. That year also marked the start of the Glen Eden Enhancement Project. An "Image Enhancement" proposal was now being considered in 1987. This would involve a number of phases including a beautiful entranceway from Eight Mile Road, new stationery and brochures, and a video interview of past Board members. However, some of this was contingent on the sale of the Farmington Hills property. New names were also being considered for new gardens.

Weather

Weather cannot be dismissed or taken lightly. While Glen Eden was blessed in 1987 in serving 853 families with interments, General Manager Press reported in 1988 the following:

> In talking about the weather, what can one say about it that hasn't already been said: HOT AND DRY. Temperatures at 90 degrees or more for 14 days during May and June, reaching 104 on June 25th - .87 inches of rain during May the driest May since 1934 and the third driest ever. These two months of above normal temperatures and below normal rainfall have caused severe ground conditions here at Glen Eden. In addition to a very poor appearance, we foresee long-term problems. Many of our trees and shrubs already show signs of deterioration and we anticipate losing many of them. Second quarters of years past have never had these serious weather conditions.

Recognition was given to Board Chairman Mr. E. Carl Fackler, Jr. (also known as Ernest C. Fackler II) for 35 years of uninterrupted service on the Board, and to Treasurer Mr. Franklin W. Schmidt for his 20 years on the Board of Directors. Their many years of devotion and dedication to Glen Eden had contributed greatly to its success.

The Board of Directors, 1987: left to right – Rev. Douglas Thompson; Mr. Elmer Engel; General Manager Mr. Richard Press; Mr. Robert Burger; Rev. Robert Baer; Mr. E. Carl Fackler, Jr., Chairman; Mr. Franklin Schmidt; Dr. Mark Halboth; and, Rev. (Dr.) Victor Halboth, Jr.

The words of Jesus: "Come unto Me, all ye that labour and are heavy laden, and I will give you rest." - Matthew 11:28

A new feature for the new **Garden of the Reformation** was being prepared for by the Rock of Ages Co. in Barre, Vermont. No new monument feature had been installed since the mid-1960's. The new feature for the Garden of the Reformation would be some form of statuary depicting Martin Luther in a distinctive pose. This seemed like a slam-dunk. However, the statuary of Luther did not come about until 1995.

Above right – One of the oldest and largest monuments in Glen Eden is a large Cross with Luther's coat of arms or crest (the Luther seal) in its center. (This monument is best seen from an aerial view, but no picture of this was located.) Unbeknownst to most cemetery visitors is what is on the back side of this monument, below right. It is a large plaque in which Luther gives a detailed explanation of his seal, the colors and their meaning.

Excursus - Pastor's Point and the Garden of the Reformation

During the days prior to and following America's Observance of Memorial Day, Glen Eden Memorial Parks adorn the graves of those who served in the Armed Forces of our nation with an American flag. All over Glen Eden there are flags in all the various gardens, but **one garden has white flags** (below) with either a general "Christian" cross or with the Luther seal (crest). These are found in Pastor's Point and the Garden of the Reformation, where many pastors of the Lutheran Church—Missouri Synod or the Wisconsin Evangelical Lutheran Synod and their wives are buried.

On the Crucifix in Pastor's Point in Glen Eden Memorial Park West (above) is a plaque (next page) that quotes Holy Scripture bearing the statement that these departed servants of the Lord Jesus Christ

"preached Christ crucified," St. Paul's words in I Corinthians 1:23. The message is simply that the Lord Jesus died to save all humanity from our sins through His crucifixion and sacrificial death. Your pastors proclaimed this message throughout their earthly ministries. In Pastor's Point are buried several pastors who served faithfully not only the parishes to which they were called but also on the Board of Directors of Glen Eden and at Annual Delegate Meetings and in many other venues of service. You honor them in stopping to pay respects at their graves, giving thanks to Almighty God for their service. A side note: How Pastor's Point got its original name is unknown throughout their earthly ministries. In Pastor's Point are buried several. Re-name it? No, the name seems here to stay.

The Garden of the Reformation recalls the voluminous work of Martin  Luther, the Great Reformer, who sought to return the Church to its central focus on the Jesus Christ and justification by God's grace through faith in Christ as taught in Holy Scripture. The large statue of Luther is at the center of the Garden of the Reformation, which was dedicated on October 22nd, 1995. He has an open Bible so that people might hear, read, learn, and take to heart the Word of God.

Lutheran Hour Speaker Rev. Dr. Oswald C.J. Hoffmann was the Guest Preacher. A huge amount of publicity was given for this event. This Dedication was the highlight of 1995.

The watchwords of the Reformation:
Sola Gratia – Sola Fide – Sola Scriptura – Sola Christus – Soli Deo Gloria

"God is our Refuge and Strength, a very present help in trouble…" --
Psalm 46:1
(Scriptural basis of Luther's hymn, *"A Mighty Fortress"*)

☙

Chapter 6

Farmington Hills Property Sold – Glen Eden Starts a New Era with an Enhanced Image

The decade of the 1990's anticipated a new millennium. Would the 21st Century be a "brave, new Orwellian world?" People of saving faith in the Lord Jesus Christ knew that their God was and is a God of infinite mercy and grace. They could look to their Savior from sin and live in the hope that the Gospel of our Lord exudes. And so it would begin for Glen Eden Memorial Park and her caretakers. **The '90s were the decade of the technology explosion.** Simple home computers, mere play toys, were giving way to desk-tops, I-pads, and cell phones for far more than simple communication and gaming, but now also for business, research, and the way education would be done in schools and institutions of higher learning.

Significant events were playing out also on the world and domestic stage. East and West Germany were reunited after the fall of the Soviet Union. Boris Yelstin became Russia's first elected President, only to be succeed in the next decade by Vladimir Putin and an eventual return to "Cold War" dynamics, which was thought to have died with the 1990's. The United States became involved in the First Gulf War (Operation Desert Storm) in Iraq and Kuwait. A more moderate Democrat, Bill Clinton, was twice elected to the Presidency. He proclaimed the new computer age something that would bring all manner of benefits to America. We've since learned that digital technology would have its serious pitfalls, including scamming and pornographic indulgence, later to be succeed by its offspring, so-called artificial intelligence, within two decades. Cloning and stem-cell research would take the human race into dangerous waters, with even General Motors getting involved in genetic engineering. The Detroit Red Wings won Stanley Cups in 1997 and 1998. Many termed the decade a very good one, some even saying it was the best decade ever with the economy booming and pop culture taking center stage. However, the LGBTQ and gay lifestyles would pose a militant and blatant assault on biblical teaching and the Church's call to repent of such sinful behavior.

Here is an interesting chart of Glen Eden Lutheran Memorial Park's performance from 1987 to 1997 (est.), relative to Michigan burials:

MICHIGAN (MI) DEATHS – ANALYSIS OF MARKET SHARE

	1987	1988	1989	1990	1991	1992	1993
	1994	1995	1996	1997 (estimate)			
A) MI Deaths	79,795	80,075	78,566	78,501	79,738	78,916	82,281
	82,646	83,405	83,496	82,994			
B) MI Cremations	11,872	12,386	12,497	13,431	14,775	15,866	17,460
	18,244	17,529	17,800	19,336			
C) Wayne County Deaths	22,525	22,414	21,822	21,409	21,186	20,857	21,455
	21,349	21,267	20,607	20,200			
D) Glen Eden Burials	853	843	773	743	759	713	745
	822	787	804	833			

Glen Eden and its Board of Directors was and is not about analytical numbers per se, since each death in the world involves a blood-bought soul, purchased in the sacrifice of our Lord Jesus Christ on the Cross of Golgotha almost 20 centuries ago, which is priceless. Each committal in Glen Eden represented not just a human being who died – hopefully and prayerfully in the Lord – but a family grieving and in need of God's grace, comfort, and peace. However, the Board, in service to them, must also pay attention to the grave, mausoleum crypt, and urn spaces available in the Memorial Park and to what was happening in the world, in the nation, in Michigan, and in greater Detroit as this cemetery ministry continued into this context into the 1990's and the next century.

Excursus – Wildlife at Glen Eden

Glen Eden Lutheran Memorial Parks are just that, "parks." Though primarily places of repose for the dead and peaceful and quiet places for the living to reflect and remember family and friends, the Parks are also tranquil places for birds and animals. Although Glen Eden West in Livonia has the largest park area, the other Glen Eden parks also enjoy the presence of wildlife. For this excursus, though, we'll focus primarily on Glen Eden's west campus.

Among the animals one can frequently or occasionally see in the Park are squirrels of various colors, chipmunks, deer, rabbits, groundhogs, an occasional skunk, fox, and, by the ponds and creek, leading from the big pond and heading east, turtles and birds of all kinds. Canadian geese, families of ducks of varying kinds, swans, cranes, and other birds are noticeable much of the year. Of the Office staff, Lee Wilson remembers seeing a family of coyotes cross over Eight Mile Road from Glen Eden.

Glen Eden's southern boundary in Livonia is with Whispering Willows Golf Course and Livonia's Bicentennial Park, which is a virtual wildlife preserve. Across the street (Eight Mile Road) is Farmington Hills Founders Sports Park, where wildlife is also to be found.

Besides the cranes, geese, and ducks, one can see and enjoy all manner of other birds in Glen Eden Lutheran Memorial Park West. There are the usual robins of Spring, sparrows, chickadees, blue jays, finches, cardinals, blackbirds, and an occasional woodpecker, hawk, or crow. Eagles have also been sighted in the Park. Veteran grounds worker Maurice Cupp once saw a bald eagle land on top of the Chapel Mausoleum. Lovely butterflies are often flitting about during the warmer seasons. The key to seeing some of God's lovely creatures is to come when the Park opens early in the morning, or, depending on the season, just before closing. In Summer and Winter, this author has seen the deer in small herds, including large bucks, does, and fawns, as well as large gatherings of ducks and ducklings on the ponds. The gift of a Memorial Park is that it is a quiet place of God's acre for reflection and seeing His beauty and love in His creation.

"As a deer pants for flowing streams, so pants my soul for You, O God. My soul thirsts for God, the living God" - Psalm 42:1

The first half of 1990 saw the granting of free graves in Pastor's Point to the Rev. Martin W. Mueller and his wife, Betty. Though not a pastor of long-standing in the greater Detroit area, Pastor Mueller was the founding pastor of Holy Redeemer Evangelical Lutheran Church (English District-LCMS) in Sandusky in the Michigan thumb, having carried out a distinguished career, including having been Editor of *The Lutheran Witness*. His wife, Betty, was for many years the Editor of the English District's monthly newsletter, *The English Channels*, and also served as Editor of *The Detroit Lutheran* until its closure in the 2010's. Pastor Mueller had also served a number of vacancies and filling-in around the Detroit area.

The fate of the old office building was sealed with the completion of the new Administrative Office Building on the opposite side of the entrance roadway. On March 30th, 1991, the old building was leveled, the debris removed, and the hole was filled in and graded as to the terrain, with sodding and new trees to come later.

> *"It is good to give thanks to the Lord, to sing praises to Your name, O Most High; to declare Your steadfast love in the morning, and Your faithfulness by night…"* - Psalm 92:1-2

Dedication of the Arch and Office Building

As part of the Enhancement Project, both the Arch and Entranceway and the new Administrative Office Building were dedicated on June 2nd, 1991, to the glory of God and the benefit of Glen Eden Lutheran Memorial Park. This was the day of the Dedication and Patriotic Memorial Observance. General Manager Richard Press reported that more than 100 were in attendance to sing hymns of praise and participate. A U.S. Navy color guard opened and closed the ceremonies while a pianist and trumpeter providing music for the Service.

From the previous page – Right below: A recent picture of the Office Staff (named on page viii & ix) in front of the "new" (1991) Administrative Office Building.

Left below: The flags of the United States, state of Michigan, and the "Christian flag," in front of the Office Building.

Left, this page: A lovely but older picture of the entrance-way off of Eight Mile Rd.

Meanwhile, 812 more niches were added to the Mausoleum. The market value of the Farmington Hills property for sale was now in 1991 at $3,970,000, but still not sold.

Finally in 1992, Glen Eden Lutheran Memorial Park was able to sell its Farmington Hills property, of some 85 acres to the City of Farmington Hills. Why the acreage changes? In order to sell the property, 20 additional acres needed to be purchased in two 10-acre parcels. Only one of them was procured. After years of interested parties, some coming up with "winning" bids but unable to secure financing, the City of Farmington Hills concluded it wanted the valuable land for a sports park. And that it what it is today, complete with soccer and baseball fields, boche ball, tennis, basketball, volleyball, and basketball courts, an outdoor skateboard track, an ice arena, and a nature trail. Founders Sports Park is now 101 acres and a treasure to area residents and guests.

Glen Eden Memorial Park would, in the years ahead, become multi-sited, with locations in Macomb Township in Macomb County at 26 Mile Road, at the Lutheran Church of the Redeemer in Birmingham (a columbarium) in Oakland County, and a new Glen Eden in St. Clair County on Fred Moore Highway, east of I-94. The Boards of Directors and General Managers would steer the good ship of Glen Eden Lutheran Memorial Park(s) into new directions rather than enlarging the main campus of Glen Eden Memorial Park West.

Over the course of decades, Glen Eden's Board continued to increase salaries and benefits. The Board members were and still are non-salaried volunteers. The Rev. Victor F. Halboth, Jr. was now Chairman of the Board of Directors. "Vic" made sure - with his gifts of persuasion – to ensure that charitable gifts would annually be given, even during periods of financial struggle.

On May 13th, 1996, Glen Eden held its **third annual golf outing for funeral directors** at Western Golf and Country Club in Redford Twp. 49 golfers teed off. The event was well received. At this time, big financial ticket items for Glen Eden were capital improvements. These had been made regularly, judiciously, but intentionally and future-focused. Interest rates, switching banks, and investments were carefully reviewed quarterly by the Board. In late August of 1996, the Board and General Manager Press were looking toward a major loan for further mausoleum expansion. Glen Eden was now also engaged in an "Outreach Project," with the hiring and training of two new sales representatives to reach 450-plus churches and funeral homes with literature and any needed services from Glen Eden. The literature featured the new Mausoleum expansion.

The end of 1997 marked a sad chapter in Glen Eden's history and a parting of the ways with the General Manager and his firm. Yet Glen Eden would continue in its godly service to families and the Detroit metro area as a Lutheran cemetery open to Christians of all faiths. Approval was given for a contract the L.F. Sloane Consulting Co. for temporary management of Glen Eden Lutheran Memorial Park. At this

time, **Mr. Craig Zitterman was given the title of Director of Operations (Grounds Superintendent)**. [Years later, he would follow Mr. Thomas Habitz as General Manager, the two then having a long and very fruitful working and friendship relationship. Mr. Zitterman is pictured, left, on the job in August, 2023, during the construction additions on St. Gabriel Mausoleum]. Early in 1998, three candidates were presented for the position of General Manager. **Mr. Thomas Habitz, Sr., was elected as Glen Eden's new General Manager.** In early 1998, Glen Eden's Total Assets stood at $16,006,563 with a General Fund Balance of $8,331,170. The Perpetual Care Fund Market Value as of December 31st, 1997 was $5,248,938, and the Building and Development Fund Market Value was $4,984,115. General Manager Tom Habitz was glad to report in June that sales for the first five months of 1998 had increased significantly.

In 1998 there was an inquiry regarding the cemetery of St. Peter Evangelical Lutheran Church of Macomb, Macomb County. In time, this would result in a new Glen Eden Memorial Park. Maintenance of individual churches' cemeteries would start to begin to become an issue, especially for declining congregations, for the next few decades. The year of 1998 ended calmly.

The Last Year of the Millennium, 1999

A bit of perspective. The faithful General Manager, Grounds Superintendent, and Glen Eden office staff and grounds personnel always start a year, under God's grace, in the earliest days of January. The Board of Directors, on the other hand, begins its formal work together at the first Board meeting. Other than the calling of a special Board meeting, the first meeting normally would be in March or April.

However, Board members would work in committees or individually with the General Manager, especially the Chairman and the Secretary, even at the start of a new year. 1999 began with a time of productive visionary thinking and exchange of ideas. This was occasioned by contacts with St. Peter Evangelical Lutheran Church and School in Macomb, which had a cemetery and 40 adjacent acres. However, there was another site of 40 acres, a little further to the north, also possibly available. Also, in March of 1999, it was suggested that Glen Eden develop a mission statement.

At the April 23rd, 1999 Annual Meeting of Glen Eden Lutheran Church, held at Western Golf & Country Club, Redford Twp., 104 delegates and guests were in attendance. This was the largest attendance to date at a Corporation Association Annual Meeting. Ms. Kathy Mueller was new to the Office Staff in 1999, and she is still working diligently and faithfully in 2023. Further discussions took place regarding a possible Glen Eden site on Romeo Plank Road in Macomb County, though concern was expressed for Glen Eden taking on more indebtedness to accomplish this. The Board, though, went out to take a look at the property and have a dinner meeting with pastors and congregational chairmen to determine how much support really existed for a Glen Eden East..

Like many cemeteries, Glen Eden had significant indebtedness as a result of Mausoleum expansions and other developments and maintenance. Board member Fred Zehnder gave a report as to **how to liquidate most of the $2,200,000 debt.** All the funds except $100,000 each, were taken from out of the three Church extension fund accounts. The Bank would still be asked for a $500,000 line of credit. It was understood that when larger revenues would allow, the Church Extension Funds would be restored. At this time, white marble benches could also be purchased; later this would be revoked since grass-cutting is made more difficult by having "obstacles" like park benches.

The selling of **Estate Lots** at Glen Eden West and the selling by Glen Eden of burial vaults now became a reality. In a charitable gesture of concern for people of limited financial means the Board approved having 100 spaces allotted for at-need burial services at a modest cost.

The Board also approved the "construction" of a Glen Eden website (**glenedenmemorialpark.com**.), just in time for the 21st century! Burials and cremations were also up over 1998. However, with more and more churches starting to erect columbariums, the question was raised as to whether Glen Eden should get involved.

What almost was overlooked in the flurry of Board activity in 1999 was the Dedication of the third phase (second addition) to the Mausoleum, which now had three chapels in it, a larger original Chapel and two smaller ones. The Guest Preacher for the Dedication on October 3rd, 1999, was the Rev. Dr. Wallace (Wally) Schultz, Associate Speaker of the Lutheran Hour. The event had great press coverage in the *Detroit Lutheran*, thanks to Editor Betty Mueller.

Mausoleum-Chapel of Memories

Below: Outside and in back of the Mausoleum-Chapel. Picture (left) taken from near the other mausoleum, the St. Gabriel Mausoleum, and looking at the connecting Plaza waterfall feature, which contains outdoor urn niches on both sides. Picture (right) of the large plaque cenotaph in the

Mausoleum-Chapel are the biblical words of Jesus in the Gospel according to St. John: *"This is my commandment that you love one another..."* John 15:12

The Family Estates section of Glen Eden Lutheran Memorial Park West represented a change in policy in allowing standing monuments to a certain height, since previously burials were only with a flat ground-level grave marker.

"As a father shows compassion to his children, so the Lord shows compassion to those who fear Him. For He knows our frame; He remembers that we are dust. As for man, his days are like grass; he flourishes like a flower of the field; for the wind passes over it, and it is gone, and its place knows it no more. But the steadfast love of the Lord is from everlasting to everlasting on those who fear Him, and His righteousness to children's children, to those who keep His covenant and remember to do His commandments."
– Psalm 103:13-18

Chapter 7

A New Millennium and a Leap of Faith – The Beginning of Glen Eden East

"From the rising of the sun to its setting, the name of the Lord is to be praised." - Psalm 113:3

Great excitement and expectations, coupled with global warming and other concerns, marked the changing of the calendar from December 31st, 1999, to January 1st, the year of our Lord 2000. May readers of this book will both solemnly and humorously recall the night a new millennium began. While there were those who would argue that the new millennium would begin on January 1st, 2001, most folks and now history has recorded that January 1st, 2000 marked the beginning, and a new era in human history.

The first decade would carry with it events that stagger the mind, including "9/11," the September 11th, 2001 Terrorist Attack on the United States of America. But more on that later.

For Glen Eden, with the Dedication of the second addition (third phase) of the Mausoleum, Glen Eden now had three chapels of varying sizes and design:

- ❖ The Chapel of Memories – the largest, and part of the original Mausoleum-Chapel
- ❖ The Garden Chapel – on the direct opposite side of the Chapel of Memories, with a magnificent faceted glass wall separating the two chapels, viewable from other side, and
- ❖ The Rose Chapel – part of the 1985 addition, featuring a Luther rose (crest) faceted-glass window.

Considering that far more entombment, inurnment, and interment services were being held in the chapels than at graveside, the value of having these three chapels was clear. Later, another mausoleum, the St. Gabriel Mausoleum, was added. St. Gabriel has no formal chapel, but there is a moveable altar.

Still more was being added to Glen Eden Lutheran Memorial Park West honoring life. A small but lovely monument in the Providence Hospital Memorial (below left) was added in 2002. This monument honors the memory of children who did not live to birth. The St. Mary-Mercy Newborn Memorial (below right) is on the opposite side in the area of roadways directly behind the mausoleums. This equally lovely monument was added in 2020 to honor life given infants who have died. (St. Mary-Mercy Hospital was renamed in 2023 as Trinity Health System.) These Roman Catholic hospitals uphold the sanctity of life is upheld, here partnered with Glen Eden's own Lutheran strong pro-life stance. The annual Sanctity of Human Life March at Glen Eden (in January or June) begins at these two monuments, ending at the memorial in the Garden of the Lambs.

Providence Hospital Memorial   **St. Mary-Mercy Newborn Memorial**

As the new year, decade, century, and millennium began in the Year of our Lord 2000, the major item on the agenda was whether Glen Eden Lutheran Memorial Park should expand to the east side of greater Detroit. To shorten a long story, approval was given in 2004.

But meanwhile, a **Memorial Day Observance** – more fitting by nature of the occasion - was held at Glen Eden Lutheran Memorial Park West **on Sunday, May 20th, 2001. The guest speaker was Retired General John W. Vessey**, a Missouri Synod Lutheran, who was the 10th Chairman of the Joint Chiefs of Staff. Having had such previous luminaries as guest speakers, it was only fitting that the former highest ranked military officer in the country, now retired, serve as the Guest Speaker. This was a tremendous honor for Glen Eden and the good General. The Color & Honor Guard of American Legion Post 32 of Livonia served in the Memorial Day Observance, as well.

September 11th, 2001

General Vessey's visit to Glen Eden was all the more significant when, a few months later, **deadly terrorists attacked the United States on September 11th, 2001**, a day that will forever be remembered by those living at that time and told to younger generations. Four planes were hijacked by Islamic terrorists. Two were crashed into and destroyed the twin World Trade Center Towers in lower Manhattan in New York City. Another was crashed into the Pentagon in Arlington, Virginia. Another crashed into a Shanksville, Pennsylvania field, having been diverted from its San Francisco destination to head toward and destroy the Nation's Capitol. Almost 3,000 people were killed and thousands more injured. The nation was shaken to the core. Every American was affected in heart, mind, and spirit by this horrific terrorist attack against the United States, resulting eventually in the Iraq War, the capture and execution of Saddam Hussein, and finally killing of the

9/11 mastermind, Osama bin Laden. September 11th, is now called in America **"Patriot's Day,"** but it is commonly referred to as "9/11".

This attack caused numerous changes in American life. A Department of Homeland Security was formed. TSA (Transportation Security Administration) became a ubiquitous security force at American airports. Airports all of the world installed security checkpoints, even as terrorists still attempted to hijack airplanes and other forms of mass transit. For some time, people were afraid to travel. Security measures by Homeland Security were hugely increased. For a few brief weeks, depending on the locale, church attendances soared as people sought the Lord God for answers and meaning amid this tragic event and aftermath.

The cataclysmic event of September 11th, 2001, affected the leadership of Glen Eden Lutheran Memorial Parks, as it did every American, resulting in erecting a monument in front of St. Gabriel's Mausoleum that honored First Responders and the Military.

Following after Glen Eden's earlier reports of records of Michigan deaths through 1997, the following was reported:

MICHIGAN (MI) DEATHS – ANALYSIS OF MARKET SHARE

	1998	1999	2000	2001	2002 (est.)	20-Year Average
A) MI Deaths	84,906	86,835	86,988	86,250	86,500	81,687
B) MI Cremations	22,925	24,197	25,938	27,291	28,500	16,859
C) Wayne County Deaths	20,248	20,763	20,267	20,171	20,250	21,336
D) Glen Eden Burials	819	855	855	**882***	870	803.

* all-time high

This data, coupled with that of 1987-1997, shows the following:

- No surprise, cremations were rising dramatically across Michigan and for Glen Eden.
- Wayne County deaths were increasing, but slightly.
- Glen Eden's number of burials had finally peaked (2001).

What the cold, hard data does not show is what Glen Eden truly stands for: ministering to families at the time of the deaths of loved ones, and continuing to be a place of peace, comfort, and rest for the living and the dead.

Glen Eden Lutheran Memorial Park East in Macomb was now becoming a reality, with a new marketing plan underway. On January 14th, 2003, Mr. Tom Habitz attended a seminar for Lutheran pastors, sponsored by Glen Eden, with the Rev. Dr. Dale Meyer, Lutheran Hour Speaker and later President of Concordia Seminary, St. Louis, as the featured speaker, a highly-gifted, relational, and engaging orator. The pastors gave thanks to Glen Eden for the event. It gave General Manager Habitz the opportunity to thank them for their support for Glen Eden East. Again, Glen Eden helped sponsor Council of Lutheran Women's Annual Luncheon (of Greater Detroit) at Burton Manor, Livonia, on January 21st, with over 1,100 women (and a few men) in attendance. Our General Manager appreciated being introduced to the assembly, giving Glen Eden great visibility.

Around this time, a poem, titled *"This Is A Cemetery,"* was found in the files of loose Minutes, and to which we would add:

> **A cemetery like Glen Eden Lutheran Memorial Park is a place of healing, grace, and peace with God, the Author of life, Whom, through saving faith in our Lord Jesus Christ, will bring His own to the place of our greatest longing, the heavenly Eden, Paradise.**

An all-time record 122 delegates and guests attended the Annual Meeting of Glen Eden Lutheran Church of Glen Eden Lutheran Memorial Parks on April 23rd, 2004. It was held at Western Golf and Country Club in Redford Twp. As usual, Board Chairman Rev. Victor Halboth, Jr., D.D. introduced the members of the Board of Directors and Mr. Thomas Habitz, General Manager of Glen Eden. He in turn introduced the office staff, sales staff, and members of the grounds crew. Mr. Habitz joyfully announced that the first purchases of graves at Glen Eden East had taken place. A total of $51,000 of charitable gifts was given at the Annual Meeting. This amount has varied from year to year as budgeted.

On Sunday, June 13th, 2004, the Dedication of the new Glen Eden Lutheran Memorial Park East in Macomb and opening of the new Office took place. In time, a beautiful Chapel would be erected (pictured on previous page). Glen Eden was once again in two counties, but farther removed from each other, with the main office being in Livonia, Michigan. Construction of the new St. Gabriel Mausoleum at Glen Eden West was begun in the Summer, and Glen Eden was awarded the Lutheran Business of the Year by Historic Trinity Evangelical Lutheran Church. Again, Glen Eden received the Beautification Award from the Eight Mile Rd. (Boulevard) Association.

The Year of our Lord 2004 ended, having witnessed the sale of 47 acres of Glen Eden West in Livonia to Golf Ridge Properties, LLC. The selling price was $4,080,000 and would eventually result in 118 detached, high-end condominiums. Also of significance, **Mr. Ray Saylor** retired on December 24th, 2004, having served on the Maintenance Staff of Glen Eden for over 34 years and for many years as Grounds Superintendent. He and his wife retired to Tennessee.

A Columbarium was also being added to one of the Glen Eden Association member churches, the Lutheran Church of the Redeemer in Birmingham. It would be owned and managed by Glen Eden in a collaborative arrangement, with details still being worked out with the Birmingham City Planning Commission.

$51,000 was budgeted for regular charitable gifts given each year by the Glen Eden Lutheran Church Association. However, due to the purchase of the property to begin Glen Eden East, resulting in major indebtedness, and rapidly rising oil prices in 2005, the amount given in charitable gifts in 2005 was decreased to $36,000. In the next years, with worsening financial conditions in the nation, especially in the "Great Recession" of 2007-2009, and especially in 2008, Glen Eden Lutheran Memorial Parks were also affected. Financial belt-tightening was the order of the day.

The Financial Report ending December 31st, 2004 showed Glen Eden Lutheran Memorial Parks' Assets at $28,557,557. Compare Assets at end-2004 with that of 1995 ($11,926,810) and 2000 (18,411,229), each year posting a similar or significant increase.

Whenever a new cemetery is opened, it takes some time before families take advantage of it to bury their loved ones. Yet growth for Glen Eden East would slowly come. By this time, Glen Eden West had seven full-time grounds workers. But with increasing cremations, there were then fewer traditional burials. At this point, Glen Eden had indebtedness of $5,000,000, but with a plan to amortize it over a seven-year period.

A Time of Dedications

Over one hundred people were in attendance for the June 13th, 2004 Dedication of **Glen Eden Lutheran Memorial Park East**. The new **St. Gabriel Mausoleum** at Glen Eden West was dedicated on May 29th, 2005, having a capacity for 648 crypts and 656 cremation niches. The Dedication of the **Glen Eden Columbarium at the Lutheran Church of the Redeeme**r in Birmingham, with General Manager Thomas Habitz and Rev. Victor Halboth, Board Chairman, participating, was November 6th. The Columbarium is owned and managed by Glen Eden Lutheran Memorial Parks, but the property it sits on is owned by Redeemer Congregation, Birmingham, hence a collaborative relationship. The Board of Directors' Meeting of December 2nd, 2005 was in the Boardroom at Glen Eden East in Macomb Township. By the December 8th, a year later (2006), Mr. Habitz happily reported that a $20,000 sale at Glen Eden East occurred the previous day.

By the end of 2006, the statewide cremation rate in Michigan had risen to 38.01%, up from just over 19% in 1997. Both Michigan and the United States as a whole continued to show the upward trend of cremations. Something new was the "hits" on Glen Eden's website. By 2007, the Glen Eden's website "hits" averaged about 2,600 per month. But to further strengthen Glen Eden Memorial Parks' visibility in the greater Detroit area, a TV ad campaign was launched in January, 2008 on Channel 7, WXYZ-TV news at 12:00 noon on Mondays and Tuesdays, with the offer of discounts. Also in 2008 at Glen Eden East in Macomb, new upholstery was added to the Mausoleum and re-landscaping of the front entrance and in the Garden of Innocence.

"But You, O Lord, are enthroned forever; You are remembered throughout all generations." - Psalm 102:12

Excursus – Involvement in the Community

Over the decades, the members of the Board of Directors, General Managers, and Staff have been involved in the community and the Church-at-large. These leaders have not squirreled themselves off in a corner but rather deeply care about the communities in which they serve. Memorial Services at Glen Eden have been a part of the Memorial Parks' ministry almost since the start of the cemetery. What was once an Annual Memorial Day observance close to the U.S. holiday and weekend of Memorial Day is now an Annual Memorial Service at Glen Eden Lutheran Memorial Park East and semi-annual Memorial Services at Glen Eden West, as well as an annual Sanctity of Human Life March and brief outdoor Service.

Here are some of the organizations in which Glen Eden General Managers, Board members, and/or Staff and spouses have had or currently have membership and involvement:

- MCA (Michigan Cemeteries Association)
- NCA (National Cemetery Association)
- ICCFA (International Cemetery, Cremation & Funeral Assoc.)

- Livonia Chamber of Commerce
- Redford Township Chamber of Commerce
- Lutheran High School Association Board of Directors (BOD)
- Lutheran Men's Luncheon Club of Greater Detroit
- Council of Lutheran Women's annual luncheon
- Thrivent & Kids Coalition Against Hunger meal-packing event
- Rotary Club of Livonia and BOD
- Livonia A.M. Rotary Club and BOD
- MOST Ministries Board and mission trips
- Lutheran Special Education Ministries (LSEM) BOD
- Livonia Public Schools Early Literacy Volunteers (tutoring)
- Seedlings Braille Books for Children
- Livonia Civic Chorus
- Numerous Lutheran Church--Missouri Synod and Wisconsin Evangelical Lutheran Synod boards and committees, and local and state chaplaincies including:
    English District Board of Directors (LCMS); LCMS Board for International Mission; Concordia University-Ann Arbor Board of Regents and Advancement Committee; Michigan Lutheran Seminary and College Board of Directors in Saginaw (WELS); Concordia Seminary Board of Church Relations.

In recent years, a Sanctity of Life Service and March has been sponsored by two LCMS pastors (Revs. Rennie Kaufman and Sam Watters). The event participants literally "march" (walk) from the two hospital children's memorials to the Garden of the Lambs and its Divine hand and baby monument dedicated to the sanctity of life in loving memory of the innocent victims of abortion. It was originally held on the anniversary of the tragic January, 1973 Supreme Court ruling of Roe vs. Wade, nationally legalizing abortion, the murder of the unborn in their mother's womb. This was at the coldest time of the year. When the Supreme Court overturned Roe vs. Wade 50 years later, the annual event was moved to the month of June to honor that ruling. Pastors Sam Watters and Rennie Kaufman again led a brief Service and March, with around 60 in attendance.

Below: A small part of the group still left after the March for Life. Glen Eden Board member, Weldon Schwiebert, is tall and in bright blue.   June 24th, 2023.

ognie

Chapter 8

The Changing Nature of the Cemetery Business: Glen Eden Makes Improvements, Reaching By God's Grace

The previous chapter mentioned what was changing during the late 1990's and into the 2000's, namely the rapid rise in cremations. This was true not only in Michigan but throughout North America and Europe. The voices of pastors and theologians who raised religious objections to cremation were largely ignored, and even within the confessional Evangelical Lutheran church bodies. Their voices, if raised, were largely muted. What may have seemed shocking to some was the number of LCMS and WELS pastors who – upon dying in the Lord – were cremated, whether at the family's choosing or their own expressed wishes.

Yet Glen Eden Lutheran Memorial Parks – now with fewer actual burials or entombments – continued to serve the greater Detroit community and make improvements. General Manager Thomas Habitz, as Michigan Cemetery Association President, courageously testified before a Michigan State Senate sub-committee regarding pending legislation regarding cemeteries. He also noted that Glen Eden hosted three luncheons for church senior groups, all in relation to Glen Eden Lutheran Memorial Park East. His presence over the years and in 2008 at numerous luncheons, conferences, pastoral gatherings, Chamber of Commerce meetings in Livonia and Redford Twp., and other events was capped off with his being honored as the **2008 Year Lutheran Layman of the Year** at the April 27th Banquet of the Lutheran Men's Luncheon Club of Metro Detroit, held at the Ukrainian Cultural Center in Warren.

At this time, Glen Eden's Board of Directors was meeting annually at least once at Glen Eden Lutheran Memorial Park East. The total number of burials (interments, entombments, and inurnments) for the seventh straight year declined to 737 (down from the all-time record high of 882 in 2001). Clearly, cremations without an inurnment in Glen Eden's cemeteries or Michigan cemeteries were playing a major role in the overall decline of "burials." Glen Eden had now contracted in 2008 "…with CBS Outdoor Sign Company to provide six months of advertising on a digital billboard located at the intersection of M-59 (Hall Road) and Van Dyke, receiving eight seconds of ad exposure every minute of the day, twenty-four hours per day/seven days a week." Glen Eden's maintenance workers were now unionized. The union contract was negotiated by Glen Eden's attorney, Mr. John Entenmann, for a two-year extension of their present union contract. There were minimal legal expenses. In addition, Glen Eden had now hired a Director of Community Relations, focusing on the Macomb Twp. Glen Eden East location.

Have you heard of the **"Red Flag" rule?** It concerns identity theft and with social security numbers and other personal information. It requires firms to create a written Identity Theft Prevention Program (ITPP) designed to identify, detect and respond to "red flags" - patterns or specific activities - that could indicate identity theft. The ICCFA (International Cemetery, Cremation and Funeral Association) had encouraged Glen Eden to adopt this rule. To be in compliance with federal regulations, the Board approved this rule.

Mr. Larry Sloane shared a proposed "Revenue Enhancement Program: Lutheran Cremation Service." While this proposal for a cremations services enhancement program was something innovative and 'out of the box,' the Board of Directors decided against it.

Several grounds improvements were made at both Glen Eden West and East. Again Glen Eden Lutheran Memorial Park West was one of 16 out of 1900 businesses selected for the **Beautification Award** in 2010 by the Eight Mile Boulevard Association. Glen Eden won this award in six out of the last seven years. (See next page)

"And the Lord God planted a garden in Eden... And out of the ground the Lord God made to spring up every tree that is pleasant to the sight...." - Genesis 2:8-9

Mr. David Brunning of Karpus & Karpus (Glen Eden's CPA since 1998), faithfully and very professionally gives quarterly Financial Reports to Glen Eden Board of Directors. In 2010, he informed the Board that Glen Eden Lutheran Memorial Parks revenues were down by 6% for the year as compared with the preceding year. However, operating expenses were also 3.5% under budget, and a positive cash flow resulted in a decrease in the bank line of credit. **Financial belt tightening was still the order of the day, remembering that the economy took a plunge in 2008.**

Now, however, in 2011, General Manager Habitz proposed a Cremation Garden. Financially, at this point, 2011 was a good year for Glen Eden. Glen Eden East was also picking up considerably in terms of the number of committals and services. Though much smaller than Glen Eden West, today it is fully a part of Glen Eden Lutheran Memorial Parks. Glen Eden East has its own Pastor's Point, as well as several small gardens. Only 14 acres are currently in use, but to the east and south is the additional acreage intended for future use. It should be noted that Glen Eden East also has a grounds caretaker and an on-site sales agent. A short-lived *Glen Eden Memorial Park Newsletter* in its September, 2011 (vol. 2, issue 2) invited recipients of the Newsletter to a Second Annual Memorial Service in December, 2011. Explaining Glen Eden as a cemetery this praiseworthy statement appeared: **"Glen Eden is a history of people, a perpetual record of yesterday and a sanctuary of peace and quiet today. Glen Eden exists because every life is worth loving and remembering – always."**

At Glen Eden East, as at Glen Eden West there is a garden that upholds Glen Eden's belief in the sanctity of human life. Our cemeteries remember children who died at an early age and those who died as a result of abortion. The lovely statuary to the right says it all in the Garden of Innocence.

The Pastor's Point at Glen Eden Lutheran Memorial Park East is smaller than the one at Glen Eden West, but it is located with a lovely view of Our Redeemer Chapel. Above left: The interior of Our Redeemer Chapel, with columbarium and, through the doors, into the mausoleum.

For the Glen Eden Memorial Parks, the cremation vs. burial rate was now close to a 50/50 percentage. This justified and gave good hope for the future utility of the new cremation **Garden of Grace at** Glen Eden West (below). This garden has now become quite popular for interments and inurnments.

The Cremation Garden at Glen Eden West became a reality and was named Garden of Grace. It is located between the creek and Pastor's Point. It was developed in two phases.

It was true that Glen Eden East for its first decade had, from a business standpoint, been under-performing. The property was being managed by Elmwood Cemetery in Detroit. In the succeeding years, the Glen Eden Board of Directors would find that Elmwood was not truly advancing Glen Eden East, since the cemetery infrastructure had not been maintained and was in need of major repair work. The Board would ultimately reclaim the management of Glen Eden East under the one umbrella of Glen Eden Lutheran Memorial Parks under the direction of General Manager Craig Zitterman. Also to help the cause, some acreage of Glen Eden East was sold off, and a few unused acres of Glen Eden West were also sold, some earlier for the development of the City of Livonia's adjacent golf course. By way of humor, Board members tried but did not get the requested free golf privileges from the City of Livonia.

The first year of a **Glen Eden Fund Appeal** in 2017 proved very successful. By October 20th, the Glen Eden Fund donation program had risen to 269 donors and $26,460. The annual appeal has continued to the present. The time of closure to Mr. Tom Habitz' long and fine tenure as General Manager was now approaching. With

Board approval, Mr. Craig Zitterman was now being trained to eventually succeed Mr. Thomas Habitz in the GM position.

By way of U.S. history, 2017 marked the conclusion of the eight-year Presidency of Democrat Barack Obama. In a highly contentious and divisive national election in November, 2017 Mr. Donald Trump defeated former Senator and Secretary of State Hilary Clinton in the electoral college vote, sending a Republican back to the White House. The nation would become even more divided politically and on moral issues such as the sanctity of human life vs. abortion; women's, minorities' and LGBTQ (gay) rights; biblical, historical, and traditional marriage vs. gay marriage; governmental spending and taxation; and, other issues, Even with a strong support base, President Trump would stir up the anger of the media and liberal groups and causes, especially in tweeting and calling out his opponents, especially as the media exploited what he termed "fake news." Overturning the Affordable Care Act (termed Obamacare and approved by Congress in Obama's Presidency) and tax reform were high on President Trump's agenda. Women's rights and white supremacist rallies were dividing the nation even further. Sadly, mass murders and shootings were increasing across the United States and internationally. 2017 and 2018 continued more of the same, but with added warnings about global warming amid increasing numbers of hurricanes and typhoons, severe weather, and drought conditions.

Amid all this, **Detroit was starting to get back on its feet** after the disastrous mayoralty of Mr. Kwame Kilpatrick, who was sent to jail. The city of Detroit, through the efforts of major philanthropist billionaires and a new mayor who believed in the city, saw new buildings on the rise, a renewed strengthening not only of the downtown core of Detroit, Corktown, New Center, and the Jefferson Ave. corridor, but also with a new Little Caesar's Arena, and further strengthening of the arts, music, and downtown culture. Under the administration of **Mayor Michael ("Mike") Duggan** (Detroit's 75th mayor), a city that was bankrupt and with 40,000 abandoned homes, was being brought back. Duggan, a one-time Livonia resident, won election as a white businessman and politician with a broad-based coalition in a city with an 80%-plus black population. He and his administration have been responsible for landing major employers to the city and vastly lowering the jobless rate. Urban blight was attacked. Parks and street lighting were restored, police presence was increased with more officers. Although Detroit still has a high amount of poverty, the loss in population has slowed. Areas have seen regentrification with an influx of new, young people moving into the city. This certainly must have been in the conversations of Glen Eden Board members and staff, city and suburban congregational members, and pastoral conferences and pastors' circuit winkels (meetings and gatherings).

Back to Glen Eden Lutheran Memorial Parks. As usual, fee increases were approved in 2017 and went into effect in 2018, comparable to other cemeteries. Glen Eden's financial position continued to improve, coupled with some interesting data concerning Michigan deaths and Glen Eden. See selected data from the chart below: * estimated

	2008	**2011**	**2014**	**2017***
Michigan Deaths	88,272	89,472	93,529	97,000
Michigan Cremations	37,269	44,054	50,944	56,000
Wayne Co. Deaths	18,795	17,937	18,003	18,400
Oakland Co. Deaths	9,408	9,652	10,320	10,640
Glen Eden Memorial Parks (total)	737	716	670	700 (actual)

This data revealed what was already known, namely, that Glen Eden's "market share" per Michigan deaths and Wayne/Oakland County Deaths had decreased to 0.72% and 2.41% respectively. Glen Eden was not alone. Over the past three decades the huge trend toward cremations meant that less people were opting to have their relatives' ashes placed in cemetery columbaria or in-ground burials. However, total number of website visits remained strong.

It was becoming clear that people once again need to learn that our bodies are not refuse to be disposed of but temples of God the Holy Spirit and whose mortal remains deserve a permanent place of remembrance for future generations to visit. Glen Eden, with a strong biblical respect for life and its sanctity was in a good position to teach (explain) the importance of interments, entombments, and/or inurnments of departed loved ones in a cemetery or memorial park over against a culture that was showing decidedly less respect for and honor of the body, even in death.

Did you know that the two most visited days at Glen Eden Lutheran Memorial Parks are on Mother's Day and Memorial Day? Perhaps that is no surprise. General Manager Tom Habitz noted that he had office and grounds staff available to assist families from 9:00 a.m. until 2:00 p.m. Over a thousand attended on Mother's Day and Memorial Day combined in 2008.

Screen fencing was also placed along Eight Mile Road on the eastside frontage of Glen Eden West. General Manager Tom Habitz further announced to the Board his intention to retire on December 31st, 2018. Grounds Superintendent Craig Zitterman shared a "General Manager Training" check list, as he was being prepared by Mr. Habitz for the GM position. Glen Eden Website visits hit their highest number to date in May, 2018: 910 "hits.", of which 84% were new visitors.

A Bylaw change indicated that the Perpetual Care Fund may alternatively be referred to as the "Endowment Fund," with the Board retaining the power to direct the funds of the Endowment Fund as deemed appropriate. The Board grieved deeply as they remembered **the death of their Chairman, Rev. Dr. Vic Halboth, on November 18th, 2018.**

> "Therefore, since we are surrounded by so great a cloud of witnesses, let us also lay aside every weight, and sin which clings so closely, and let us run with endurance the race that is set before us, looking to *Jesus*, the founder and perfecter of our faith, who for the joy that was set before Him endured the
> ***cross***,
> despising the shame,
> and is seated at the
> right hand of the throne of God."
> Hebrews 12:1-2

The Changing of the Guard

Left: retired (Tom Habitz, Sr.) **Right: on the job (Craig Zitterman)**

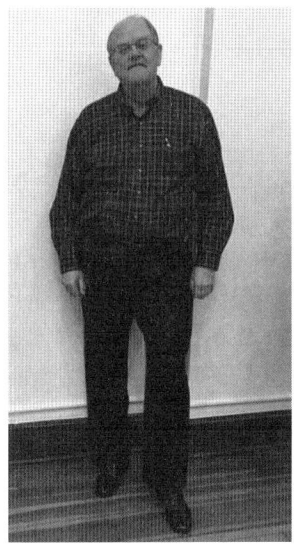

With the retirement of Mr. Thomas Habitz as General Manager (1998-2018) on December 31st, 2018, the baton of General Manager leadership of Glen Eden Lutheran Memorial Parks was now passed on to Mr. Craig Zitterman, who had served as Grounds Superintendent, 1993-2019. Mr. Zitterman continued in the role of both General Manager and Operations (Grounds Superintendent) until he brought on Mr. Greg West (2019-present) as Grounds Superintendent. Also, Mr. Habitz continued in a part-time role of continued training of Mr. Zitterman in the huge responsibilities of General Manager, assuming some of the public relations and PR Committee meetings, which was among Tom's forte. It was a very smooth transition, which in many organizations is not always the case.

With the death of Glen Eden's long-term Board member and Chairman, Rev. Dr. Victor ("Vic") Halboth, Jr. on November 18th, 2018, an era had ended. Vice Chairman, Mr. Ernest C. ("Ernie") Fackler III, was quickly made the new Board of Directors' Chairman.

Excursus – The Halboth Family – Another Family's Legacy of Dedication

Some people seem to be "larger than life." This is a kind epitaph for a man who served Glen Eden Lutheran Memorial Parks with great distinction, **the Rev. Dr. Vic Halboth** (Victor, Jr.). He was born December 21st, 1932, and baptized in Yuba City, California, where his father, Rev. Victor Halboth, Sr., was serving as Pastor. After the move to Michigan and Grace Lutheran Church, Redford Twp., young Vic was soon off to the pre-seminary Concordia Junior College, Milwaukee, and then Concordia Seminary, St. Louis. "Vic," as he was lovingly called by so many friends, vicared under the sainted Rev. Paul Boriack, at St. John Evangelical Lutheran Church, Rome, New York. There he met his wife, Blanche; they married in 1956.

Blessed with two sons, Dr. Mark and Rev. Tim Halboth, they moved, after Seminary graduation in 1957, to Redford Twp., where he and his father saw explosive numeric growth of that congregation to be the largest church in the English District-LCMS in the early 1960's. At Grace, Vic served as Assistant, then Senior, and, after "retiring," as Assistant Pastor **at Grace,** a total of 61 years. He affectionately called Grace Lutheran Church *"the anchor of north Redford,"* after the Detroit riots of 1967 and the huge ethnic change in Redford over the next few decades. Under the grace of God, he faithfully proclaimed Jesus Christ as Savior and Lord anywhere and everywhere, and the Lord used him as the "Gospel's glue" that held Grace Church together during turbulent years of racial turmoil and synodical fighting during the 1970's LCMS "Seminex era."

He was especially known in our circles as **a Board member of Glen Eden Lutheran Memorial Parks for 30 years, serving as Board Chairman for 26 years until his death**. He was so involved with Glen Eden, especially in terms of public relations and visibility in the local and greater Detroit community. His older son, dentist **Dr. Mark Halboth** (retired in 2022) of Awesome Dental Care in Livonia, and a University of Michigan graduate and ardent football fan, pictured right, began serving on the Board of Directors in 1988 and continues to serve today, bringing huge plain-spoken, institutional knowledge of Glen Eden as well as financial acumen and cigar-smoking wisdom. He is part of a family dynasty of service to Glen Eden Lutheran Memorial Park, full of stories; one of a handful of Glen Eden dynasties that have brought caring service to many people and the community.

Pastor Vic Halboth, though, was a beloved pastor of keen intellect, enormous pastoral heart and had an interest in people of all sorts, and a beloved, folksy preacher. He related extraordinarily well with people, and they with him. He simply loved people. He served for years on Redford Twp. Community committees, as Chaplain of the Michigan State Police for over two decades, as well as at Botsford-Beaumont (now Corwell) Hospital in Farmington Hills, MI, and the English District Board of Directors in the 1970s. He staunchly worked to keep Grace Lutheran Church in the English District and LCMS at the time of the synodical "split." Pastor Vic Halboth died in the Lord in 2018 after a long battle with cancer. His funeral was at his beloved Grace Evangelical Lutheran Church in Redford Twp. on Grand River Ave., with his long-time friend whom he mentored in the English District, Rev. Dr. David Stechholz, serving as preacher and **members of**

the Glen Eden Board serving as pallbearers. The funeral and committal were on Saturday, November 24th, 2018. He, along with wife, Blanche, are entombed at Glen Eden West in the Mausoleum-Chapel on the top row to the right on the main entrance. Nearby is a plaque that his fellow Board members had authorized and dedicated on Sunday, August 30th, 2020, pictured to the right.

※

2019 began with Spring Clean-up at Glen Eden Lutheran Memorial Parks, including Winter burials and memorial markers. General Manager Emeritus Tom Habitz was elected to another three-year term to the Board of Directors of the Michigan Cemetery Association. (Humor: He just never could get out from under those meetings of the MCA, of which he had been President. Certainly a grave under-taking.) On a lighter note, Glen Eden's credit card processing company was changed to Allegiance from Blue Pay, saving over $250 a month in fees. This also resulted in greater credit card security. It was also good to know that our investment portfolio was rebounding in 2019 from 2018.

The Kaiser Estate

Glen Eden Lutheran Memorial Parks was named as the beneficiary of the estate of Dr. Calvin Kaiser worth around $2 million with the stipulation that a new cemetery would be built and operated near the city of St. Clair, Michigan. This very generous bequest from Dr. Kaiser would eventually be such a blessing from the Lord God and would result in Glen Eden-St. Clair, a third Glen Eden Lutheran Memorial Park. The Board accepted the "Devises of Calvin Kaiser's Last Will and Testament," dated February 7th, 2013.

$24,000 was distributed in charitable gifts at the Annual Meeting of Glen Eden Lutheran Church, held Friday evening, September 27th, 2019, at Andiamo's Restaurant, Livonia. Yet in the years that followed, amounts would again increase. For Glen Eden, committals in 2018 (646) and 2019 (612) had reached recent low levels. Would there be a rebound in 2020? 2019 ended with an international health nemesis which began in Wuhan, China, and which would become a worldwide pandemic. It would affect all life on planet earth.

The COVID-19 Virus and the early 2020's

Early in 2020, with the Western world becoming increasingly more secularized, immoral, and more narcissistic, the deadly, highly-infectious **COVID-19 pandemic** began spreading around the world. Most of the United States, was shut down to the public. Schools, universities, and churches were closed by mid-March in 2020. International and domestic air travel came to a grinding halt. Large industries such as the automotive industry in greater Detroit were closed, resulting in billions of dollars of lost revenue. Most businesses retreated onto the 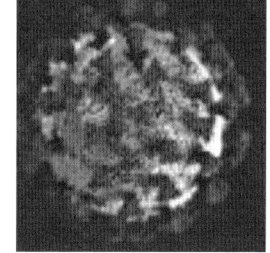 web. People were becoming gravely-ill or dying as the viral pandemic spread. Masks were required in food stores, hospitals, and places of public gathering or worship. Some churches reopened as early as Ascension Day in late May, 2020, rejecting what they considered governmental overreach to the stay-at-home orders and governmental violation of the First Amendment freedom of worship. However, most churches stayed closed for another month or two and resorted to streaming their worship services via the internet. When people returned, far less in number, many found that their church leaders had taken pains to ensure their safety through various hygienic and social-distancing measures. It took a couple of years before things returned to some measure of normalcy. By April 2022, over 500 million people across the globe had been infected. More than 6,000,000 people died from the virus (pictured above). Government responses to the pandemic were controversial and proved divisive. Businesses slowed down or folded during the pandemic, which led to a recession.

Amid the pandemic, civil unrest resulted from the killing of George Floyd, an African-American man, by a police officer in Minnesota. Over the next few months, there were many protests across the United States against police violence and racism. The Black Lives Matter demonstrations were often violent, reminiscent of the Detroit and other similar riots in 1967. Communities and police departments were on edge. Also, during 2020 and 2021 people around the world received COVID-19 vaccines. By the end of 2021, over four billion people had received at least one vaccine dose, and many a vaccine booster.

The chaotic presidential race of 2020 resulted in the unseating of President Donald Trump by former Senator and Vice President Joseph Biden. Trump refused to concede, railing against what he claimed were rigged ("stolen") elections. Trump tried to find additional votes, strongly urging Republicans who had supported him to find votes to unseat "fake electors" to the Electoral College. He called on his supporters, many of whom came to Washington, D.C. on January 6th, 2021, and some attacking and storming the Capitol building. Many were later arrested, convicted, and sent to jail. As of Fall, 2023, charges have been filed against former President Trump and 18 alleged co-conspirators for seeking to overturn the 2020 national election.

In addition, the United States pulled out of the war in Afghanistan, leaving it to immediate take-over by the Taliban. Further, the world was torn asunder by the invasion of Ukraine by Russian President Vladimir Putin's military in February, 2022. That war continues, now with vast Western and United States military aid to Ukraine, as of late November, 2023. In this period from 2020 to 2023 and continuing, the world was also becoming increasingly distressed over climate change – termed global-warming – with severe earthquakes, hurricanes, tornadoes, monsoons, unprecedented flooding, and poor air quality.

Another major event struck the world. On October 7th, 2023, Hamas Islamic militants struck Israel with explosive drone missile strikes, precipitating major conflict in their taking of hostages. Israel declared war on Hamas, striking back and bringing total destruction to Palestine's Gaza Strip. Iranian-backed Islamic militants attacked Israel and United States military posts and ships, even in international waters. Demonstrations, including on college campuses, then occurred all over the globe, whether pro-Israel or pro-Palestine. Almost two million Palestinians have been displaced, with thousands killed in Israel's war against Hamas.

Amid all this world-wide pandemonium and domestically in the U.S.A. and state of Michigan, **Glen Eden Lutheran Memorial Parks entered 2020 under God's grace and becoming increasingly aware of the spread of COVID-19 and its impact.** The Board of Directors' Meeting and the Annual Meeting of Glen Eden Lutheran Church, scheduled for April 24th, 2020, were postponed, though a "virtual" Board meeting was held. When the Board met on June 26th, some of the Board members wore COVID masks; by the next meeting, only one was masked. Yet the work of Christ's Church through the ministry of Glen Eden Lutheran Memorial Parks continued, especially that of helping families laying to rest their loved ones.

Even during the year of the viral pandemic, Glen Eden did well financially in the first quarter, and by the end of the second quarter, almost 400 families had been served. This faithfulness to serve was and is one of the things that sets Glen Eden apart. Glen Eden went the extra mile, even amid the pandemic, to help and serve families in their hour of need for committals of loved ones. Other cemeteries put burials on hold. General Manager Craig Zitterman even set up a system for tracking churches of the deceased that had services at the church before their committal service. Our General Manager was also securing contractors to "covid clean" (sterilize) the buildings on the St. Clair property.

Mr. Christian Habitz, Glen Eden's investment advisor, gave us the good news that the market was starting to rebound. However, he then shared the bad news that J.P. Morgan, with whom Glen Eden had their investments, was withdrawing from working operating companies, especially church-related entities such as Glen Eden.

Mr. David Brunning, CPA, in giving a Financial Report, noted that the Endowment Fund was now valued, as of December 31st, 2019, at $8,068,812, a decrease over the previous year. However, the first half of 2020 was a remarkable half-year in terms of profits and losses. Mr. David Mammel, Board Treasurer, announced that in handling the legal matters connected with the estate of the late Calvin Kaiser, Glen Eden was soon to receive an additional check of $525,000, in addition to the $250,000 already received. Also, by the end of 2021, Board member

Pastor Stechholz was glad to report that 62 congregations had been visited. They received materials for their churches and were willing to put up Glen Eden posters. The added Church newsletter and Service bulletin paragraph information were supplied by Glen Eden.

The St. Mary-Mercy Hospital (now Trinity Health) Newborn Loss Memorial had been dedicated on October 14th, 2000, and the first burials took place in the Spring of 2021. New Family Estate lots were completed. The new Brookside Garden's section with upright monuments was also completed and grave lots were being sold. In a report on the Kaiser Estate it was stated that the whole new Glen Eden St. Clair project was to cost about $600,000.

The nation was shaken to its core with the January 6th, 2021 assault on the Capitol building in Washington, D.C. The ramifications of this deadly attack, even while some meant it as a peaceful protest of the 2020 presidential election results, would go on for years. Yet Glen Eden Lutheran Memorial Parks would continue in its service to the Christian community of greater Detroit. New as a guest presenter to the Board of Directors was Mr. Michael Neaton of One Digital, the new investment advisor. He explained his investment goals for Glen Eden as a portfolio of 60% stocks and 40% bonds. He was seeking to keep Glen Eden's funds liquid and reduce fees from approximately $150,000 to about $40,000. Mr. David Brunning also reported that Glen Eden was now on a good financial trend. The Board also mutually agreed to the development of the Glen Eden St. Clair Memorial Park by selling off unneeded property.

COVID caused the cancellation of the Board of Directors' and spouses' annual Christmas holiday dinner party in 2020. The Board, which is not paid for their volunteer work and extensive hours of service, are at least treated to an annual "gift" of a wonderful Christmas party arranged by Mrs. Charla Halboth, wife of Dr. Mark Halboth. So in 2021, we were blessed with two such "holiday" parties, one in December, but preceded by the "2020 Christmas dinner" in August at Fleming's Steak House in Livonia.

A large bell, currently in the possession of History Trinity Evangelical Lutheran Church in Detroit, was noted by Chairman Ernie Fackler. It was generally agreed that the bell should be incorporated into some future tower or new building at Glen Eden West.

Calvin Kaiser's wish was becoming a reality as a brand new 10-acre cremation cemetery was being developed on Fred Moore Highway in the town of St. Clair. At the same time, in the Summer of 2021, the management contract between Elmwood Cemetery and Glen Eden Lutheran Memorial Park East expired. Glen Eden was again assuming management of Glen Eden East in Macomb Twp. Hence the relationship with the L.F. Sloane Consulting Group was ended, and new employees were on site. Mr. Zitterman also reported to the Board, first, that the Family Garden Estate project at Glen Eden West was now completed and very successful in terms of sales; and, second, that Glen Eden West had now opened the new **Orthodox Garden of Remembrance** with both flat granite and upright monument markers.

$48,000 was distributed to several organizations as Glen Eden charitable gifts for 2021. Now two women's pregnancy centers on the west and east sides of Detroit, both upholding the sanctity of human life and helping women in crisis pregnancy situations, were being aided, as well as a one-time-only $10,000 Glen Eden Special Emergency Fund for Church Emergencies. In late June, 2021, greater Detroit was devastated with the flooding from torrential rainstorms. One church in particular, Zion Evangelical-Lutheran Church of Detroit, sustained millions of dollars by the flooding of the Church undercroft, including the closet containing very expensive vestments and paraments; the rented-out School gym and classrooms; and, the Church's Rectory/Parish Hall basement and the Pastor's library. Receiving two $2,000 gifts was such a blessing and was acknowledged by Father Mark Braden, the Pastor, and Mr. Thomas Habitz, Jr., the Congregational Chairman. Two other congregations - St. Matthew's, Westland, and St. John's, Fraser, MI, also had storm-related damage, and received $3,000 each.   MOST (Mission Opportunities Short-Term) Ministries out of Ann Arbor, an LCMS RSO (recognized service organization) was now also added to the list of organizations receiving a charitable gift.

Michigan's deaths rose dramatically from 2019 (99,095) to 110,000 (estimated for 2020), due to COVID-related deaths. Glen Eden had also served 710 families with committals in 2020, up significantly from 2019. As part of the Annual Meeting packet, included was **the Mission** Statement of **Glen Eden Lutheran Memorial Park(s),** with the tagline "*Where Families of Faith Remember Christ's Promises.*" The Mission Statement reads as follows:

Glen Eden Lutheran Memorial Park, operated by a community of Lutheran churches, will serve each customer individually and fully with Christian care and the highest standards of excellence. By serving each customer, one at a time, Glen Eden will fulfill its vision of being the premier provider of bereavement services. Such levels of service, coupled with prudent management of the fiscal and physical resources of the cemetery, will ensure its religious, cultural, historical, and environmental importance perpetually.

Friday evening, June 3rd, 2022, just prior to the Annual Meeting, the **new Crucifix at Pastor's Point** was dedicated, Bishop Emeritus Stechholz conducting the Dedication rite, and with the assistance of Pastor Greg Gibbons. The Annual Meeting was on a beautiful, pleasant day and held under a large rented tent in front of the Mausoleum-Chapel. The previous 2021 Annual Meeting had been held later than normal, on October 21st, 2021. (The COVID had caused this later-than-normal Annual Meeting.) However, at this June 3rd, 2022 Annual Meeting, attendees were treated to Glen Eden West at its finest, many taking the opportunity to view the memorial park and the mausoleums. Comments were received, such as: *"We had no idea that Glen Eden was so beautiful!"*

Attendees heard General Manager Craig Zitterman talk about the planned additions to the St. Gabriel Mausoleum and eventually providing an additional 288 badly-needed crypt spaces and 1,300 granite-fronted niche spaces for urns on the north and south sides of the building. He also told the delegates that Glen Eden St. Clair was now opened, with the first sale recorded on May 18th.
He finally mentioned that Glen Eden's Board of Directors and his staff were now working with Mr. Curtis Jackson of Digitalliance, a local Birmingham marketing and advertising firm with vast cemetery experience with the Mt. Elliott Cemeteries. Again, $48,000 in charitable gifts were presented under the outdoor canopy at Annual Meeting and Banquet, with two new recipient groups added: Cares and Cares in Farmington Hills and Livonia Cares.

The Board approved a new logo and branding for Glen Eden Lutheran Memorial Parks. Attention and slight variations were given to the three different memorial parks –
  Glen Eden West,
  Glen Eden East, and
  Glen Eden St. Clair.

Excursus – The Habitz Family – And Still Another Family's Dedication to Glen Eden Lutheran Memorial Parks

Even with the retirement of **Mr. Thomas Habitz, Sr.,** as General Manager (1998-2018) at the end of 2018, the Habitz footprint in Glen Eden Lutheran Memorial Parks is huge. Tom not only mentored his successor as General Manager, Mr. Craig Zitterman, but he also continued for another year after retirement as an advisor and consultant to Mr. Zitterman and the Board.

Mr. Habitz continues to serve on the Glen Eden Public Relations and Marketing Committee, and his wisdom and advice is sought not just by General Manager Zitterman and the Board of Directors, but also by Chairman Ernie Fackler and the author of this book. It should be remembered, though, that Mr. Habitz was preceded in service to Glen Eden by his father, **Mr. Arthur W. Habitz, Sr., who served on the Board of Directors** (1973-1981). Tom's sons, Tom Habitz, Jr., and Brent Habitz continue to show keen interest in Glen Eden, having been the "Habitz boys" Glen Eden grounds workers for six Summers. For many years, Tom Jr. has been the lay delegate to the Annual Meeting of Glen Eden Lutheran Church from Zion Evangelical-Lutheran Church of Detroit, where he serves as Congregational Chair. It is also salutary to remember the accomplishments and events during Mr. Thomas Habitz Sr.'s era as General Manager of Glen Eden Lutheran Memorial Parks as follows:

- 1999   Dedication of third part of Glen Eden Mausoleum & Fountain Plaza (directly behind the Mausoleum)

- 1999 The selling of Estate Lots at Glen Eden Lutheran Memorial Park West
- 2000 The entrance of Glen Eden into a new millennium
- 2001 Approval by the Board to start Glen Eden Lutheran Memorial Park East in Macomb County, Michigan
- 2001 The terrorist attack on the United States (now known as 9/11)
- 2003 Glen Eden honored, recipient of the 8 Mile Road Blvd. Assoc. Beautification Award (won again many times in years following)
- 2004 A record 122 delegates, staff, and guests attend the Glen Eden Annual Meeting
- 2004 Dedication of Glen Eden Lutheran Memorial Park East in Macomb Twp.
- 2004 Sale of 47 acres of Glen Eden West property to Golf Ridge Properties, LLC for 118 detached condos for $4,080,000
- 2005 Dedication of Glen Eden West's second mausoleum, the St. Gabriel Mausoleum
- 2005 Dedication of Glen Eden's Columbarium at the Lutheran Church of the Redeemer, Birmingham
- 2008 Tom Habitz Sr. honored as Lutheran Layman of the Year by the Lutheran Men's Luncheon Club of Metro Detroit, having also served on their Board
- 2013 Dedication of the Garden of Grace (cremation garden) at Glen Eden West
- 2015 Dedication of the new Luther Statue at Concordia University-Ann Arbor, with Habitz having being instrumental in helping CUAA get Luther statue
- 2018 Training of Mr. Craig Zitterman as successor

Beyond this timeline, Mr. Habitz as General Manager worked with some challenging personalities and through some difficult financial times. He worked diligently with the Board in helping the fledgling Glen Eden Lutheran Memorial Park East to grow, receive new monuments and gardens, and not to give up on Glen Eden East when it was hemorrhaging money. Tom was especially noted for his tremendous public relations skills, serving on numerous Boards and Committees, as well as being President of the Michigan Cemetery Association, and attending countless community, church, pastoral conferences, and other events, spreading the good name of Glen Eden far and wide. In all this, Tom Habitz, worked closely with his Grace Lutheran Church Pastor, Rev. Dr. Victor Halboth, Jr., the Chairman of Glen Eden's Board of Directors. In short, Mr. Thomas Habitz lived out a family legacy of service to Glen Eden.

"Into Your hands I commit my spirit; You have redeemed me, O Lord, faithful God." - Psalm 31:5

Mausoleums

Glen Eden East   Glen Eden West

Chapter 9
A Near Century of Service

The Glen Eden Columbarium
at the Lutheran Church of the Redeemer

In 2005, Glen Eden embarked on a special relationship with the Lutheran Church of the Redeemer in Birmingham, Oakland County, Michigan. With the sale of Glen Eden Lutheran Memorial Park's property directly across Baseline (Eight Mile) Road in 1992, to the City of Farmington Hills for a sports park, Glen Eden no longer had a presence in Oakland County. The goal had been to develop those original 79 acres for burials, but after years of legal wrangling with the city over tax assessments, that vision had to be abandoned. Hence, the concept of working with a large Oakland County LCMS congregation that desired to have a columbarium on its grounds  was appealing. The Columbarium was built and managed by Glen Eden on the Redeemer Church's grounds.

All seemed well for many years with the Glen Eden Columbarium on Redeemer's property. However, as the congregation grew, complete renovation of Redeemer's house of worship and relocation of the columbarium was the consecrated desire. Communication of the plan to relocate the columbarium and Glen Eden's role and financial obligation was mirky and caused a period of tension with Redeemer up to mid-2022. **The August 24th, 2005 Letter of Agreement** between Glen Eden Lutheran Memorial Parks ("Glen Eden") and the Lutheran Church of the Redeemer stated that Glen Eden would construct the Columbarium on the Church's property and "...operate the Columbarium within the rules and regulations, fee schedules and practices as approved by the Church and attached to the Agreement." In other words, there would be a close and cordial working relationship between Redeemer Church and Glen Eden.

The point at issue came when the Church approved a major reconstruction of the House of Worship and moving of the columbarium without the Glen Eden's Board's full knowledge.

After some back-and-forth efforts and meetings over a couple of years, the matter was largely resolved. Glen Eden paid the Lutheran Church of the Redeemer $88,462.50 for half of the cost of relocating Glen Eden's Columbarium on the Lutheran Church of the Redeemer's property in Birmingham, Michigan. The ownership of the Columbarium is Glen Eden's, but the property is Redeemer Church's. Niches current range in cost is from $3,500 to $6,000.

"For I know that my Redeemer lives, and at last He will stand upon the earth. And after my skin has been destroyed, yet in my flesh I shall see God…" - Job 19:25-26

Further Expansion – Glen Eden St. Clair

The Dedication of the new Glen Eden Lutheran Memorial Park St. Clair was one of the highlights of the year 2023 and is covered with pictures and comments on the next pages.

Dedicated to the glory of God and in memory of the cemetery's Benefactor, Dr. Calvin John Kaiser on Saturday, June 10th, anno Domini 2023

Pictured above, left to right: Mr. David Mammel, Rev. David Stechholz, Mr. Ernie Fackler (Chairman). Mr. Tom Habitz (General Manager Emeritus), Mr. Craig Zitterman (General Manager), Rev. Joel Baseley, and Dr. Mark Halboth

Calvin Kaiser's earthly remains are under the pictured marker (above) that one sees upon entering the new memorial park. The monument marker is between the two flagpoles at the entrance.

Pictured below at the Columbarium at the center of the cemetery is the family of the late Calvin John Kaiser, his sister, Carol Harrell, in white, in the middle.

There is more that should be said about Glen Eden St. Clair's late and most generous benefactor, Dr. Calvin Kaiser. He was born on August 4th, 1935, and raised in Grosse Pointe Park, MI until 2008. He then moved to 2727 Carriage Lane, St. Clair, Michigan. Dr. Kaiser was Program Associate for the Detroit Public Schools in the Office of Research, Evaluation, and Testing at the time of his retirement. He was known to be honest, God-fearing and God-loving, extremely intelligent, hard-working, and talented. It was said that he would do anything for his extended family.

Glen Eden Lutheran Memorial Parks is hugely indebted to Dr. Calvin Kaiser for his extreme generosity in providing the land and the means to help make Glen Eden-St. Clair a reality. Rarely in human history is such unexpected and undeserved generosity extended to a cemetery association. Therefore, Glen Eden pays huge tribute to Calvin Kaiser and the legacy he has left, and all to the glory of Almighty God alone, through our Lord Jesus Christ.

"Create in me a clean heart, O God, and renew a right spirit within me." - Psalm 51:10

Looking to Glen Eden's Future

Writing history is not an exact science. Rarely can such an endeavor be done without recording history in some chronological order. For the more interested reader of Glen Eden's vast history, see the larger volume, **God's Acre: The History of Glen Eden Lutheran Memorial Parks**. This briefer History of Glen Eden Lutheran Memorial Parks, is also written under the title *God's Acre*, a beautiful old term for a Christian cemetery. It does not contain as many excursuses as the larger volume. Yet, in this little book, the author has tried to generally follow a chronological arrangement of the Glen Eden "story." Every effort was taken, even with small diversions, to keep the history straight. **The common thread in Glen Eden's history is God's grace in Christ**, His guiding of the General Managers, Boards of Directors, office and maintenance staffs, and the constituent congregations with delegates to the Annual Meeting of Glen Eden Lutheran Church as an ecclesiastical corporation. Hence, Glen Eden has been, is presently, and will continue to be a godly corporation, three cemeteries and a columbarium in four different Michigan counties, serving God's people with loving and caring committal of the dead to God's acre.

Annual Meetings of the Glen Eden Lutheran Church have, over the decades, morphed into a short meeting with a reading and approval of the previous year's Minutes, a series of brief reports, and other business, ably chaired by the Chairman of the Board of Directors. Introductions of the Staff and Board members are made.

The highlight has been the awarding of charitable gifts from Glen Eden to various charities and churchly organizations. The attendee-recipients of charitable gifts have come to enjoy the camaraderie of their organizations and the various work that they each do in God's Kingdom of Grace. Some do a bit of networking with each other. This godly "fellowshipping" is very affirming over against the rising tide of secularism, materialism, and anti-Christian sentiments that are weakening the fabric of our nation. Christ's Church is always a pilgrim stranger on earth. However, with our Glen Eden Memorial Parks we aim to give a Christian witness and provide wholesome service to families whose loved ones have fallen asleep (died).

Glen Eden has not yet embarked in her second century of service, but under the grace of God the General Manager and staff and Board of Directors continue to serve and guide so that our mission is not mere words but actions of love and care. It is always hard to predict the future. Certainly cremations continue to rise, even while we encourage bodily burial either in the earth of God's acre or in mausoleums. As of late Autumn, 2023, work continues on the additions to the St. Gabriel Mausoleum. The grounds crews and the office staffs are busy. Grounds maintenance, including replacing dying trees and shrubs, is ongoing. People come to the offices on a regular basis. Others use their computers or cell phones to "hit" on Glen Eden's websites. Many look on the beautiful Glen Eden website for locating the burial sites of loved ones and friends.

One of the challenges confronting all cemeteries in America is overcoming people's fear of going to burial grounds to pay respects and to recall the past. Glen Eden's marketing efforts are receiving a great deal more attention by the Marketing and Public Relations Committee and Board of Directors. One goal is simply to get people to come and visit the lovely Glen Eden Lutheran Memorial Parks and the Columbarium at Redeemer Church, Birmingham. One piece of this effort is to provide greater contact with and encouragement between our pastors and their parishioners concerning Glen Eden and the services our cemeteries provide. Another piece is to provide helpful publicity to our constituent Lutheran churches. What was done a few years ago with posters for church bulletin boards and brief write-ups quickly becomes dated and forgotten. Glen Eden's visibility in the community through service and charitable gifts also continues.

Will there be new opportunities for Glen Eden for the future? While only the Lord of the Church knows that answer, the future may not be necessarily what we hope for and desire. For example, the leadership of Glen Eden was pleasantly surprised when Dr. Calvin Kaiser willed his estate for the creation of a cemetery in St. Clair County. Our Board of Directors begins each Board meeting in prayer to the Lord, asking for His guidance and blessings. He is the Lord of the future, and Him we trust, and while we act locally, we of Glen Eden do think globally. We live in a world of 8.1 billion people, with a U.S. population as of September 8th, 2023 of over 340,341,000 people.

While the current world population growth rate has been slowing (now 0.88% over 2022) for decades, the United States continues to grow, mostly through immigration but with a lower birth rate. People (all) still die, many dying in the Lord and needing a Glen Eden.

For this moment in time, we on the Glen Eden Lutheran Memorial Parks Board of Directors, General Manager Craig Zitterman, and Staff can only but give thanks and praise to Almighty God for His abundant grace for 90-plus years and as we look to our centennial celebration. May He continue to guide and bless, giving us new vision and purpose in serving those in need with Christian care and compassion. May our Glen Eden parks be a place of refuge and peace, beauty and tranquility, even as the world turns and the Great Day of our Lord's return approaches.

Right: Lobby area in the Administrative Office building at Glen Eden Lutheran Memorial Park East, Macomb.

Our Lord and Savior, Jesus Christ, has said:
*"Let the children come to Me; do not hinder them,
for to such belongs the Kingdom of God."*
- Mark 10:14

Again, our Lord Jesus Christ says:
"I am the Resurrection and the Life. Whoever believes in Me, though he die, yet shall he live, and everyone who lives and believes in Me shall never die." - John 11:25-26

To God alone be the glory.

Soli Deo Gloria

Bibliography

Baseley, Joel R. *"Christian Burial Practices: History and Meaning,"* a pamphlet. Glen Eden Memorial Parks: Livonia, MI, 2021.

Bartlett, John. *Familiar Quotations*, 14th Edition. Toronto: Little, Brown and Company, 1968.

Concordia Historical Institute Quarterlies:
    Allwardt, Erich B. *"Death and Burial of C.F.W. Walther,"* Concordia Historical Institute Quarterly, Summer, 1987, Vol. 60, No. 2, pp. 52-64.
    Fuerbringer, Ludwig Ernst. "President's Report: *"From the Proceedings of the Thirty-Fifth Convention of The Evangelical Lutheran Synodical Conference of North America,"* Concordia Historical Institute Quarter, Vol. 96, No. 1, Spring, 2023, pp. 9-16.

Eberhard, The Rev. Dr. David, Editor. *Histories of the Lutheran Churches in the City of Detroit, Michigan.* Dau Church History Library, Historic Trinity Evangelical Lutheran Church, Detroit, Michigan, 2000.

Fredrich, Edward C. *The Wisconsin Synod Lutherans: A History of the Single Synod, Federation, and Merger.* Northwestern Publishing House: Milwaukee, 1992.

"Glen Eden Edition, The," Volume 1, No. 1. Glen Eden Memorial Park: Livonia, MI, October, 1995.

Granquist, Mark (Rev. Dr.). *Lutherans in America: A New History.* Fortress Press: Minneapolis, 2015.

Index List of Landowners (in Livonia Twp.) of Wayne County, 1876, 1902 (Index and Maps; published by the Downriver Genealogical Society (representing Southeastern Wayne County, Lincoln Park), at Livonia Civic Center Library.

Interviews, and Memorabilia and Personal Notes from the following:

    Mr. Mark Bliese, Research and Reference Manager, Concordia Historical Institute, St. Louis, MO.

Mrs. Bette (nee Wagner) Clary, a Livonia resident; baptized and catechized at Gethsemane, Detroit

Mr. Maurice Cupp, Maintenance Dept. Worker (1980-present), and **Mr. Terry Cupp**, Maintenance Dept. Worker (1985-present)

Mr. Ernest C. Fackler III, Glen Eden Board Chairman (2019-present)

Mr. Thomas Habitz, Sr., General Manager (1998-2019)

Dr. Mark Halboth, Board of Directors member (1989-present)

Rev. Timothy Halboth, Senior Pastor, Grace Evangelical Lutheran Church, Redford Twp., MI

Mr. Kenneth Ingram, life-long Zion member and Military Street, Detroit resident

Mr. Allen Kerkes, former organist, Zion, Detroit, and local Lutheran historian

Mr. Gregory Kremkow, a member of Guardian, Dearborn

Rev. Dr. Cameron MacKenzie, Jr. Professor of Historical Theology, Concordia Theological Seminary, Fort Wayne, IN, and son of long-term Board member and Board Chair, Rev. Cameron MacKenzie, Sr.

Mr. Marty Moro. Executive Director, MOST (Mission Opportunities Short Term) Ministries, Ann Arbor, MI

Mr. Craig Zitterman, Grounds Worker (1980-1993), Superintendent (1993-2019), and Glen Eden General Manager (2019-present)

Lutheran Cemetery Association (Glen Eden Lutheran Cemetery Association) Minutes of the Board of Directors and LCA Delegate Meetings: Volumes, 1930-1943, 1949-1971 (succeeded as Glen Eden Lutheran Church [Board] Minutes and Annual Meeting Minutes): Volumes replaced by annual binders, 1971-1983, 1986-1992, loose copies, 1992-1996, annual binders 1996-2000, loose copies and consolidated binders, 2001-2022, annual binders 2022-2023

Melville, Greg. *Over My Dead Body: Unearthing he Hidden History of America's Cemeteries*. Abrams Press: New York, 2022.

Moulton, J.H., and Milligan, G. *Vocabulary of the Greek New Testament*. Hendrickson Publishers: Peabody, Massachusetts, 2004.

Mueller, Martin W. *Amazing Comeback: Survey of English District History*. An English District Publication, 1986.

Prange, Peter M. *Wielding the Sword of the Spirit, Volume One*: The Doctrine & Practice of Church Fellowship in the Missouri Synod (1838-1867). Joh. Ph. Koehler Press: Wauwatosa, Wisconsin, 2021.

Stechholz, David P. *The English District Saga: A Niche in the History of the Evangelical Lutheran Church in North America*. Angels' Portion Books: Linden, Michigan, 2021.

The Lutheran Study Bible: English Standard Version. Concordia Publishing House: St. Louis, 2009.

Wikipedia, Information on cemeteries and historical events during periods from 1929-2023.

Glen Eden Lutheran Memorial Parks

General Managers, Grounds Superintendents, Board Chairmen, Past & Current Board Members, and Maps

General Managers

Mr. P.(Percival) B. Warr (Glen Eden Development Company and Lutheran Cemetery Association, 1930-1939)

Mr. E. (Harry) Eberlein (Lutheran Cemetery Association) General Manager (1940-1945)

Mr. Walter Keller (1945-1949)

Mr. Russel Kuhlman (1949-1950)

Mr. Harold C. Seitz (1951-1952)

Mr. Harold R. (Hal) Biesel (1952-1955)

Mr. Alvin C. Meyer (1955-1984)

Mrs. Nancy Stebbins (brief, 1984)

Mr. Richard M. Press (1984-1997)

Mr. Thomas Habitz, Sr. (1998-2019)

Mr. Craig Zitterman (2019-present)

Grounds Managers (Superintendents)

Mr. Elmer W. Garchow (1930-1943)

Mr. R.E. Schmidt (1955-1959)

Mr. William Campau (first as Acting Superintendent in 1959, then by 1962, permanent)

Mr. Henry Luker   (around 1968)

Mr. Raymond Saylor (1970??-1991)

Mr. Randy Mauck (1992)

Mr. Craig Zitterman (1993-2019) – began part-time at Glen Eden in 1982

Mr. Greg West (2019-present) – recruited by Craig Zitterman

Board Chairmen (Presidents, et. al.) and from which Church

Mr. Frederick R. Robinson,   President (Glen Eden Development Company, 1929)

Rev. Herman Metzger,   First President of the Lutheran Cemetery Association, Gethsemane, Detroit, 1930, (served later as Vice President, also as Board member, then President again)
    Additional Original LCA Officers:
Mr. Fred L. Wulf, Vice President (Nazareth, Detroit, 1930-1933)
Mr. Henry Schatz, LCA, Secretary (Zion, Detroit, 1930-1942)
Rev. W.O. Kleinhans, Treasurer (Calvary, Lincoln Park, 1930-1933), and Mr. Henry M. Martens, Treasurer (church??, 1934-1935)

Mr. Edward Meyer,   President   (Stephanus, later St. Stephen's, Detroit, 1931-1934)

Mr. Henry M. Martens, President (Calvary, Lincoln Park, 1935-1942)

Mr. William F. Fenske, President (church??, 1943-1948?)

Rev. W.E. (Walter) Rehmus, (St. Stephen's, ??-1948)

Rev. Erwin Beyer (St, Paul's St. Clair Shores, 1949-1953)

Mr. Walter Gaul (church??, 1953-1955)

Rev. Cameron A. MacKenzie (St. Matthew's, Detroit, 1955-1973)

Mr. Carl R. Thomsen (Grace, Redford Twp., 1973-1983)

Mr. E. Carl Fackler, Jr. (St. Andrew, St. Andrew-Redeemer, Detroit; Hosanna-Tabor, Redford Twp., 1983-1989)

Mr. Robert A. Burger (Emmanuel, Dearborn 1989-1993)

Rev. Dr. Victor Halboth, Jr., Chairman [President] (Grace, Redford Twp., 1993-2019)

Mr. Ernest C. (Ernie) Fackler III, Chairman [President] (Hosanna-Tabor, Redford Twp., Historic Trinity, 2019-present)

> *"Praise the Lord! Oh give thanks to the Lord, for He is good, for His steadfast love endures forever! Who can utter the mighty deeds of the Lord, or declare His praise? Blessed are they who observe justice, who do righteousness at all times."* - Psalm 106:1-3

Besides Chairmen (Presidents), Other Early Notable Past Board Members

Rev. Herman Metzger (above; BOD – 1930, 1933-1943, or later; President, 1930, 1942-1943)

Mr. Henry Schatz, Secretary (1930-1942)

Mr. Henry Martens (BOD 1933-1942, Treasurer, then President)

Rev. George O. Hildner (BOD 1936-1944 or later; Secretary, 1943; President, 1944 or later)

Mr. Elmer Engel (BOD, 1943-1996), Treasurer (1949-1972), longest serving Board member

Mr. Ernest C. Fackler, Jr. (also called E. Carl Fackler, 1953-1989), Secretary (1954-1975), Vice President (1976-1983), President (1983-1989)

2023 Board of Directors Members and General Manager, Staff and Regular Guests

General Manager: Mr. Craig Zitterman
Chairman: Mr. Ernie (Ernest Carl) Fackler III
Vice Chairman   Mr. Keith Mueller
Secretary   Rev. Dr. David Stechholz
Treasurer   Mr. David Mammel

Additional Board of Directors:
    Rev. Joel Baseley
    Rev. Greg Gibbons
    Dr. Mark Halboth
    Mr. Jay Kempf
    Mr. Weldon Schwiebert

Additional Regular Guest Presenters:
    Mr. David Brunning, CPA, Karpus, Scott, and Company
    Mr. Michael Neaton, One Digital Investment Advisors

Special Guest and Marketing/Public Relations Committee member:
    Mr. Thomas Habitz, Sr., General Manager Emeritus

Glen Eden Boards of Directors
(early years: Lutheran Cemetery Association)
Officers and Additional Directors

1930   Rev. Herman Metzger, President, St. Matthew's, Detroit
        Mr. Fred L. Wulf, Vice President, Nazareth, Detroit
        Mr. Henry C. (Harry) Schatz, Secretary, Zion, Detroit
        Rev. W.O. Kleinhans, Treasurer, Calvary, Lincoln Park
        Mr. Victor Ketterman, Christ, River Rouge
        Mr. Harry Meister, Stephanus (St. Stephen's), Detroit
        Mr. George Otte, Sales Manager

1931   Mr. Edward A. Meyer, President, Stephanus, Detroit
        Mr. Henry C. Schatz, Secretary, Zion, Detroit

Rev. H.O. Kleinhans, Treasurer, Calvary, Lincoln Park
Mr. Edward F. Gugel, Mt. Hope, Melvindale (Allen Park)
Mr. Albert L. Wier, Holy Cross, Detroit
Mr. E. Bauer, Bethlehem, Detroit
Mr. George Otte, Sales Manager

Other mini-dynasties of service at Glen Eden were those of **Rev. George O. Hildner**, serving on the Board from at least 1936 to 1944 or later; and his son, **Rev. George P. Hildner**, 1953 or earlier (in both cases, missing Board Minutes or records, 1943-1952) to 1966; and **Mr. Emil Kremkow** (Vice Chairman, 1932-1935), and son, **Mr. Edgar Kremkow**, during the same time periods, both separately serving on the Board.

1973 - A "Changing of the Guard"

1973 Mr. Carl R. Thomsen, President
Rev. Cameron MacKenzie, Vice President;
Mr. E. Carl Fackler, Jr., Secretary
Mr. Franklin Schmidt, Treasurer.
Initially elected Directors: Mr. Elmer W. Engel; Rev. Alvin E. Heumann; Rev. Gerhard Press; Mr. Ernest Sutton; Mr. Harley Wolfrom (later in 1973, several resignations)
New Directors: Rev. John M. Gagern (replacing Rev. MacKenzie); Rev. Carl Trosien (replacing Rev. Heumann); Rev. Victor F. Halboth, Jr., (replacing Rev. Press); Mr. Arthur Habitz (replacing Mr. Sutton); Mr. Richard Press (replacing Mr. Wolfrom)

1976 Mr. Carl R. Thomsen, President
Mr. E. Carl Fackler, Jr., Vice President
Rev. Victor F. Halboth, Jr., Secretary
Mr. Franklin Schmidt, Treasurer
Directors: Mr. Elmer Engel; Rev. John Gagern; Mr. Arthur Habitz; Rev. Carl Trosien. General Manager Alvin Meyer

Glen Eden Board at Topinkas Christmas 1976 Art Habitz, Carl Trosien, Al Meyer, Carl Thomsen, Fackler, Gagern, and Elmer Engel

(In picture, above, Mr. Franklin Schmidt is to the left of Elmer Engel.)

1988 Rev. Victor F. Halboth, Jr., Chairman
Mr. Ernest C. Fackler III, Vice Chairman
Rev. Douglas K. Thompson, Secretary
Mr. Franklin W. Schmidt, Treasurer
Mr. Fred J. Zehnder, Assistant Treasurer
Directors: Dr. Mark H. Halboth; Rev. Robert Baer; Mr. Bernhard Bohn; Mr. Fred Zehnder; Mr. Roy Houser

Glen Eden Board of Directors and General Manager Tom Habitz at December, 2001 Christmas Party.

"Bless the Lord, O my soul, and all that is within me, bless His holy name! Bless the Lord, O my soul, and forget not all His benefits." - Psalm 103:1-2

Glen Eden Board of Directors Annual Christmas Banquet, with our spouses, Thursday, December 7th, A.D. 2023. Missing from picture: Dr. Mark & Charla Halboth (in Florida). Charla had made the arrangements for this banquet, held at Cantoro's Italian Market and Trattoria in Plymouth, Twp.

Committals at Glen Eden (1930-present)

This portion of this book, *God's Acre*, is dedicated to the beloved memory of **Mr. Elmer Engel** (1905-1996). His grave marker is pictured on page 37. **Elmer served on the Board of Directors of Glen Eden Memorial Parks from 1943 to 1996. No one served longer.** His service over those 53 years was as a Board Member, President (Chairman), and especially Treasurer. He also chaired the Sales, Planning, and Mausoleum and Pricing Committees and was a Trustee of the Perpetual Care (Endowment) Fund. Elmer was not afraid to speak his mind and even vote opposite some or all of the Board, on occasion. His wisdom and dedication though, was admired and eulogized.

Another soul that must not be forgotten is the gentleman who served as the first General Manager for Glen Eden Lutheran Memorial Park in its infancy from 1930 to 1939, **Mr. Percival B. Warr, usually known as P.B. Warr.** He is buried in Brookside Garden in Glen Eden West, having died in the Lord in April 1939. Warr was a key figure at Glen Eden's conception, serving for both the Glen Eden Development Company (1929-1930) and the Lutheran Cemetery Association (beginning 1930). We give thanks to the Lord God for Mr. P.B. Warr's dedicated service, without which Glen Eden might not have survived during the 1930's and era of the Great Depression.

It is seemingly impossible to list all of the interments, entombments, and inurnments that have occurred over the course of almost a century at Glen Eden Lutheran Memorial Parks. **As of Holy Cross Day (†), September 14th, anno Domini 2023, they number 51,333.** These would include – each one precious in the eyes of God - those at the following places:

Glen Eden Lutheran Memorial Park West, Livonia   (50,500)
Glen Eden Lutheran Memorial Park East, Macomb Twp.   (735)
Glen Eden Lutheran Memorial Park St. Clair – St. Clair County   (2)
Glen Eden Columbarium at the Lutheran Church of the Redeemer, Birmingham   (96)
These figures were furnished by General Manager Craig Zitterman. Glen Eden keeps a running list of those for whom we have record.

The first burial in what would become Glen Eden Lutheran Memorial Park (West) was that of **Charlotte Eiden**. She was buried on January 20th, 1930, in the Garden of Rest. Apparently there was a child also buried in 1930 but not included in the count of those buried in 1930.

Rev. John M. Gugel was the only other person buried in 1930. He was interred in what became Pastor's Point. This was the result of a prior promise on May 10th, 1930, of a free grave. His son, Mr. Edward F. Gugel, served on the Lutheran Cemetery Association Board of Directors in its earliest years of the 1930's. The Rev. John Mathias Michael Gugel was born in Frankenmuth, Michigan, on March 26th, 1867, and died in the Lord in Detroit on April 25th, 1930. His native language was German. Where he served as a Pastor – probably in a German-speaking Missouri or Wisconsin Synod congregation – is unknown.

There have been a number of prominent burials, besides those already named in this book. Among them are the following:

Sidney ("Sid") Gerald Abel, Canadian Hall of Fame hockey player and general manager of the NHL Detroit Red Wings, 1918-2000
Ford R. Bryan, author and family historian, and fourth cousin of Henry Ford I, 1912-2004
George "Hully" Gee, professional hockey player with the Chicago Blackhawks and Detroit Red Wings, 1922-1972
Arthur Rahn, World War I German ace fighter pilot; in 1928 emigrated to USA; 1897-1962
Rev. Dr. Gilbert Otte, Pastor of Historic Trinity Evangelical Lutheran Church for 50 years, served 1927-1983, including during the construction of the current 1931 "cathedral" church, liturgical leader, author, historian, 1903-1983
Jack Engebretson, civic leader and former Mayor of Livonia (not deceased, but with a grave marker in the Garden of Grace.

"Trust in the Lord forever, for the Lord God is an everlasting rock."
- Isaiah 26:4

Maps

A map of Glen Eden Lutheran Memorial Park, dated 6/1/1964. The road (which the photo shows as curved but is actually completely straight) to the upper top is Eight Mile Road, with the lake, creek and bridge, with shrubbery crudely drawn in. What is not shown is the property on the north side of Eight Mile Road in Farmington Twp., Oakland County, where no burial plots and gardens had yet been developed. It is clear that the Memorial Park was still very much in the process of development, still lacking the first and then a second mausoleum. This map was to indicate which Gardens had been developed.

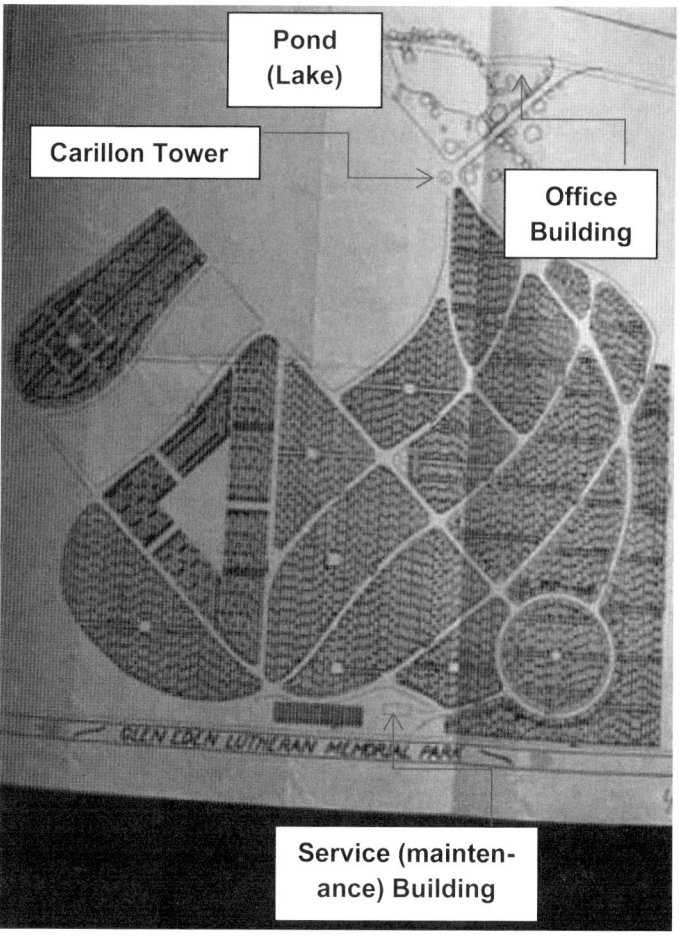

Glen Eden Lutheran Memorial Park West – Current map of Gardens

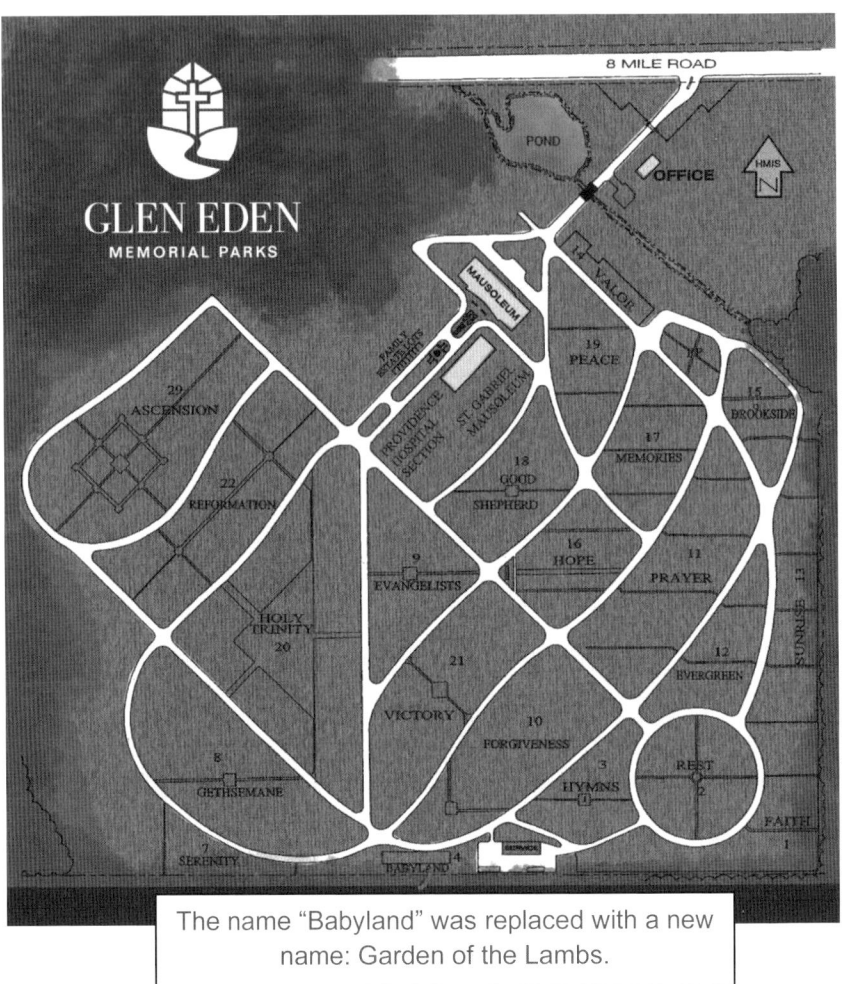

The name "Babyland" was replaced with a new name: Garden of the Lambs.

"Now faith is the assurance of things hoped for, the conviction of things not seen…" - Hebrews 11:1

SCRIPTURAL PASSAGES

Page Numbers

(*God's Acre: The Story of Glen Eden Lutheran Memorial Parks* (an Abbreviated Version)

v	Psalm 118:15	71	Psalm 92:1-2
xv	Psalm 8:1	77	John 15:12
xvi	Psalm 90:12	78	Psalm 103:13-18
xvii	Romans 6:23	79	Psalm 113:3
3	Philippians 2:9-11	86	Psalm 102:12
11	Proverbs 18:10	91	Genesis 2:8-9
27	Psalm 67:1-3	96	Hebrews 12:1-2
32	John 14:1-2, 6	110	Psalm 31:5
33	Psalm 23:1	112	Job 19:25-26
40	Lamentations 3:22-23	114	Psalm 51:10
47	Psalm 90:14	118	Mark 10:14
56	I Corinthians 15:55ff.	118	John 11:25-26
59	Psalm 34:3	124	Psalm 106:1-3
61	Psalm 1:3	128	Psalm 103:1-2
61	Psalm 90:1-2	132	Isaiah 26:4
63	Matthew 11:28	134	Hebrews 11:1
66	Psalm 46:1	136	Revelation 22:12-13, 20
70	Psalm 42:1		

A view looking northeast, upon leaving Glen Eden Lutheran Memorial Park West.

The words of the Lord Jesus Christ:

"I am coming soon... I am the Alpha and the Omega, the first and last, the beginning and the end." Amen. Come, Lord Jesus!

Revelation 22:12-13, 20